EXTINCT LANGUAGES

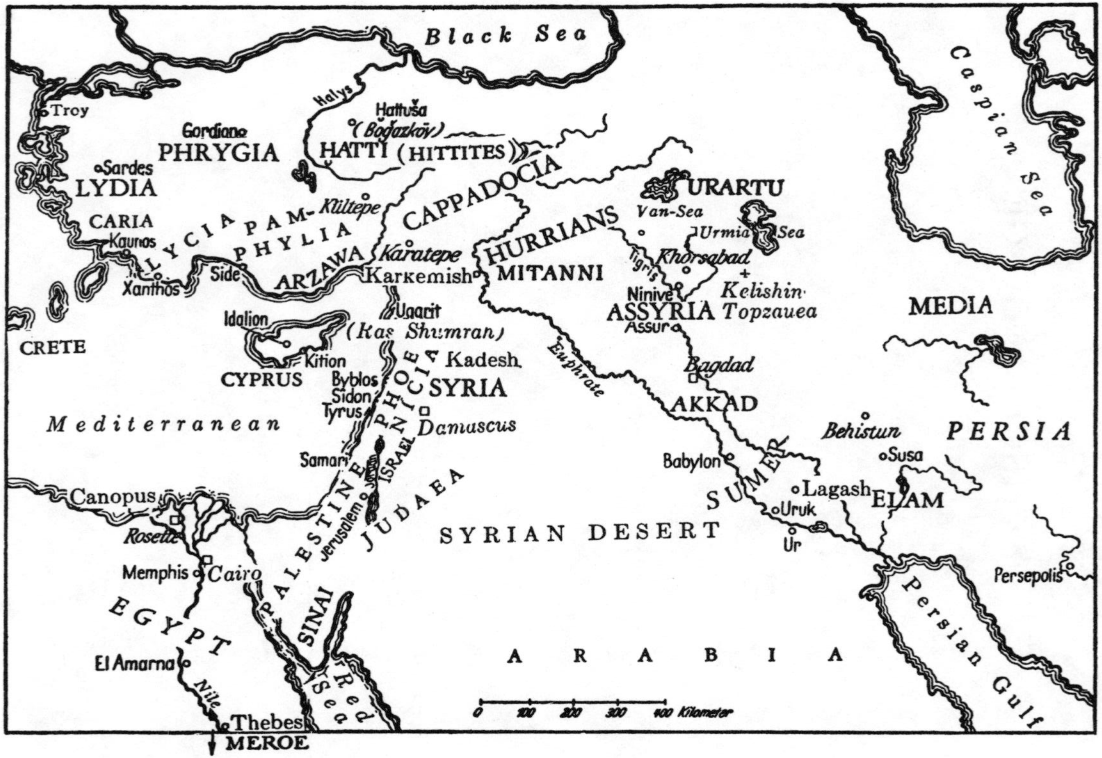
Black Sea
Caspian Sea
Troy
Gordiane
PHRYGIA
Halys
Hattuša
(Boğazköy)
HATTI (HITTITES)
Sardes
LYDIA
CARIA
Kaunos
LYCIA
PAM-
PHYLIA
Kültepe
CAPPADOCIA
URARTU
Van-Sea
Urmia Sea
Xanthos
Side
ARZAWA
Karatepe
Karkemish
HURRIANS
MITANNI
Tigris
Khorsabad
Kelishin
Topzauea
Ninive
ASSYRIA
Assur
MEDIA
CRETE
Idalion
Kition
CYPRUS
Ugarit
(Ras Shumran)
Kadesh
Byblos
Sidon
Tyrus
PHOENICIA
SYRIA
Damascus
Euphrate
Bagdad
AKKAD
Mediterranean
Samari
ISRAEL
Behistun
PERSIA
Susa
Babylon
SUMER
Lagash
ELAM
Uruk
Ur
Canopus
Rosette
JUDAEA
Jerusalem
PALESTINE
SYRIAN DESERT
Memphis
Cairo
EGYPT
SINAI
Persepolis
Persian Gulf
El Amarna
Nile
Thebes
MEROE
Red Sea
ARABIA
0 100 200 300 400 Kilometer

EXTINCT LANGUAGES

Johannes Friedrich

DORSET PRESS
New York

Translated from the original German *Entzifferung Verschollener Schriften und Sprachen* by Frank Gaynor

This edition published by Dorset Press,
a division of Marboro Books Corporation,
by arrangement with
Philosophical Library Inc.
1989 Dorset Press

ISBN 0-88029-338-1

Printed in the United States of America
M 9 8 7 6 5 4 3 2

TABLE OF CONTENTS

INTRODUCTION

In the history of human knowledge, the transition from the 18th century A.D. to the 19th is of no less a significance than is the turn of the 15th century A.D. into the 16th, which is regarded traditionally as the change-over from the Middle Ages to the Modern Era. Whereas about 1500 A.D. the discoveries and the Renaissance were reshaping the knowledge and mental attitude of mankind, the era about 1800 A.D.—quite apart from the then nascent radical shift in political thought—is characterized by a whole series of new and radical facts of knowledge, notably in the fields of the physical sciences and technology, and in connection with the latter in the technique of communications as well, which would justify the contention that in those fields the Modern Age began about 1800 A.D. This change in the natural sciences went hand in hand with a parallel change-over in various humanistic sciences. That was, for instance, the time when archaeology was given its new look, by Winckelmann, by the re-intensified study of original inscriptions, etc., and when the first steps were taken toward a true science of linguistics by the recognition of an Indo-European linguistic community, by a study of Germanic antiquity and by a systematic investigation and classification of all the recognizable languages of the world.

Another thing that happened about the same time was —and this brings me right to the topic of the present book— that the human mind began for the first time to look back at the races which had existed before the beginnings of Greek history, at the races which had shaped the earliest history of mankind in the Orient before the Greeks, at their material and abstract thinking, and at the residues of that thinking preserved in the inscribed monuments which had survived from that remote period of antiquity to the modern age. To the mind of the man of the 18th century, history had still begun, as it had for the Christian Middle Ages, with Homer and the tales of the Old Testament, and his knowledge of ancient tongues was restricted mainly to Latin, Greek, and perhaps Hebrew. Although a certain formal familiarity with the Old Egyptian monuments at least had been salvaged from remote antiquity into the modern age, the people of the 17th and 18th centuries still gazed with the same wonderment as had the Greeks and Romans at the odd pictorial characters with which those monuments were covered all over. But it never occurred either to the people of late antiquity or to those of the early Middle Ages to attempt to read this pictographic writing and to understand its contents. The knowledge of that script had been completely lost ever since it had ceased to be used. On the other hand, by today we have renewed our acquaintance with the Egyptian hieroglyphics and language, as well as with the cuneiform characters, once used in the Near East for writing a number of languages, but vanished from use and from the knowledge of mankind even earlier than the Egyptian writing, and there are also other formerly forgotten scripts and languages with which we have become re-acquainted. The scientists who contributed to these re-discoveries thus restored to linguistic science the lost knowledge of a number of languages, some of them very ancient, and they laid the first foundation on which a historical study of writing at all became possible. But above all, they expanded the historical horizon significantly toward the past. Whereas the surveyable history of mankind had formerly comprised about two and a half millennia, it was now expanded to take in at least five thousand years. And not only do the political events of those long years unfold before our eyes, but so does also the material and intellectual culture of those ancient races; their homes, their garments, their ways of living, their religious, juristic and scientific thinking come to life anew and open for us an insight into the development of human life and thought from a perspective far wider in space and time.

The decipherment of these old scripts and languages in the 19th and 20th centuries ranks with the most outstanding achievements of the human mind, and the only reason why it does not stand in the limelight of public interest as a co-equal of the radical triumphs of physics and technology and their related sciences is that it cannot produce the same effect on practical daily life which those discoveries can. This inferior evaluation is also the reason why the unlocking of the secret of extinct languages and scripts is never described coherently, and it is therefore still hardly known at all to the general public. Yet, this subject is deserving of the most careful attention of the learned minds, and is absolutely worthy of a presentation *per se*. This is the aim of the present book. I hope to be able to group the abundant material to a certain degree so as to provide a clear and comprehensive view, by first discussing at greater length the outstanding, and to a certain extent classical, decipherments of relics of the ancient Orient, that of the Egyptian hieroglyphics, of the many branches of the cuneiform writing, and of the Hittite hieroglyphics which remained enigmatic for a long time, but are now laid open to study. Next, I shall discuss, more briefly and in a looser arrangement, a few other decipherments of interest, without any attempt at completeness. Only then will I consider it proper to set forth a few theoretical reflections relative to the decipherment of extinct scripts and languages, such as follow readily from the previously explained practice. And in conclusion, I shall append the presentation of a few still undeciphered scripts, and I shall attempt to answer the query as to why they still remain undeciphered.

J. F.

I. THE THREE GREAT DECIPHERMENTS IN THE STUDY OF THE ANCIENT ORIENT

1. The Egyptian Hieroglyphics

Egypt is the homeland of the mysterious pictographic characters which even the ancient Greeks contemplated with reverent wonderment and called *hieroglyphics,* "sacred signs," because they suspected that they contained secret wisdom of the magician priests of Egypt. With the obelisks in Rome also, this notion of a magic significance of the hieroglyphics survived among the beliefs of the Occident, and also profound minds of modern times permitted themselves to be influenced by it. Without a belief in a certain mysterious wisdom hidden within the hieroglyphics, a work of art like Mozart's *Magic Flute* would be inconceivable. This is why it is fitting that a presentation of the decipherments be introduced by a discussion of the Egyptian hieroglyphics. For the sake of clarity, also a brief geographic and historical survey will be useful.

(a) *Land and People, History and Culture*

The cultural situation on African soil is rather simple; in the ancient days there was only one known civilized race there, the Egyptians whose mighty edifices and the pictographic writing on them still fill the modern visitor with no less amazement than they inspired in the ancient Greeks.

Even in remote antiquity, Egypt was known as a gift of the Nile. Only the Nile Valley, about 500 miles long but only a few miles in width, is arable land, but extremely fertile at that, nurtured by the floods of the Nile, and flanked by barren desert on both sides. The Egyptians seem to have been a race of mixed blood, of African and Semitic-Asiatic extraction; their language was a remote kin of the Semitic tongues. They considered themselves the original inhabitants of the land, and actually no other race can be demonstrated to have lived there before them.

Originally, there must have been two separate kingdoms in Egypt: A Northern kingdom (Lower Egypt) in the Delta, and a Southern one (Upper Egypt) in the narrow Nile Valley, extending all the way to Assuan, at the first cataracts. King Menes of the Southern Kingdom united both realms about 2850 B.C., and that event marked the beginning of the first of the thirty dynasties into which the Greek-Egyptian priest Manetho (about 280 B.C.) divided the entire history of the Egyptian monarchs up to Alexander. Beginning with the 3rd Dynasty, the city of Memphis, on the boundary line between the two original kingdoms (in the vicinity of modern Cairo), was the capital of the Old Kingdom. The 4th Dynasty included the great pyramid builders, Cheops, Chefren and Mycerinus, and the era of the 5th Dynasty marks the beginning of the specific worship of the sun god Re. The reign of the 6th and 7th Dynasties (about 2350–2050 B.C.) was a period of political weakness.

The Middle Kingdom introduced a new golden age, beginning with the 11th Dynasty. The city of Thebes, in the south, was the capital in those days. The political heyday of this era was represented by the reign of King Sesostris II, conqueror of Nubia (1878–1841 B.C.), and the cultural high point by his son, Amenemhet III (1840–1792 B.C.). A new decline ensued with the invasion of the Hyksos (15–16th Dynasties—about 1670–1570 B.C.), an Asiatic race of barbarians whose chief god is known to us under the Egyptian name *Šth* (*Seth*) and was a Near-Eastern weather deity.

The expulsion of the Hyksos by Amosis (1570–1545 B.C.) marks the beginning of the New Kingdom (about 1600–715 B.C.). Thutmosis I (1524–about 1505 B.C.) and above all Thutmosis III (1502–1448 B.C.) were great conquerors on Asiatic soil. Thutmosis III conquered Palestine, and in a battle at Karkhemish, at the bend of the Euphrates, he defeated the Hurrians, a race powerful in Northern Syria. Thus he created an Asiatic province of Egypt, which included Palestine and Syria and remained in existence for a long time. Also Egypt was unable to escape the influence of the highly advanced Syrian civilization; it manifested itself materially in the importation of clothes, furniture, etc., and culturally in an acquaintance with Semitic deities, such as Astarte and Baal, and in the many Semitic words incorporated into the Egyptian language.

The rule of Egypt over Syria did not last forever. Under Amenophis III (1413–1377 B.C.) and Amenophis IV (1377–1358 B.C.), Syria suffered heavily from the attacks of the Ḫabiru, an alien race of nomads, assumed to have been the Hebrews. An eloquent picture of this struggle is furnished by the correspondence of these two rulers with their Syrian vassals and with independent monarchs in Asia. This correspondence was found in the archives of El Amarna, Egypt, residence of Amenophis IV, in 1887, and to the amazement of the science of the late 19th century, it was found to have been written not in Egyptian, but in Akkadian (Babylonian), on clay tablets, in cuneiform script—because Akkadian was the language of general communication in that era.

The Egyptians soon had a new enemy to fight, the race of the Hittites, of Asia Minor, who took the place of the Hurrians in northernmost Syria shortly after 1400 B.C. Ramses I (1318–1317 B.C.), Sethos I (1317–1301 B.C.) and notably Ramses II (1301–1234 B.C.) had to fight bitter battles against the Hittites for Syria. Also the battle of Kadesh

(1296 B.C.), hailed by Ramses II in a long epic poem as a great Egyptian victory, failed to bring a final decision. Ultimately, a peace treaty with the Hittite king Ḫattušili III, preserved in an Akkadian version in cuneiform script in the Hittite state archives in Bogazköy, and in an Egyptian version in the temple of Ammon in Thebes, led to a mutual recognition of the political status quo. The long reign of Ramses II was otherwise another golden age of Egypt.

A new danger threatened the civilization of the ancient Orient about 1200 B.C.: An invasion of barbaric Indo-European races from Europe, whom the Egyptians called "Sea Peoples." Their first, and most powerful, attack completely destroyed the Hittite empire. The Egyptians were able, under Ramses III (1197–1165 B.C.), to defend their own country at least, but they irrevocably lost Syria and Palestine where indigenous Semitic kingdoms arose then. A political decline of Egypt ensued. The rule of the Ethiopian kings Sheshonk, Taharka, and others (10th–7th centuries B.C.) was followed by a short-lived conquest by Assyria (670–663 B.C.), another era of independence under the monarchs Psammetichus I, Necho and Amasis (663–525 B.C.), and then came the conquest of the land by the Persians (525 B.C.) whose place was taken by Alexander the Great in 332 B.C., and by Rome in 30 B.C.

Unfortunately, it is impossible to present here a more detailed account of Egyptian civilization; for such information, the reader is referred to *Ägypten und ägyptisches Leben im Altertum** by Erman-Ranke (Tübingen, 1923). There he will find more information on the religion of Egypt with its richly diversified pantheon of numerous, partly animal-headed, deities (Re, Ammon, Isis, etc.), its strongly developed belief in life after death (Osiris, ruler of the dead in the un-

* Egypt and Egyptian Life in Antiquity.

derworld in the west), as well as on Egyptian architecture, with the pyramids of the Old Kingdom and the great temples and pillared halls of the Middle and New Kingdoms, on Egyptian science, mathematics, medicine, etc.

(b) *The Principles of the Egyptian Writing*

The script and system of writing of Egypt are the very important cultural products which command our closer attention at this point. Let it be mentioned in this connection, first and above all, that the Egyptians were the first users of a sort of paper as writing material; it was manufactured from pressed stalks of the papyrus reed, and paper still bears the name of that reed even in our modern languages. Their writing utensil was a kind of brush, made of rushes, which they dipped into black or red ink. The direction of writing was not fixed; it seldom ran in the direction to which we are accustomed (it is merely *our* custom to print Egyptian texts mostly from left to right, for our own convenience), but in most cases horizontally from right to left, although often also from top to bottom, in which case, too, the vertical columns followed from right to left. It is to be noted that all the pictures of human beings and animals face toward the beginning of the line, also the feet walk in that direction, and the hands are stretched out so as to point that way.

About the *written characters* of the Egyptian script, it must be stated first of all, in general, that the pictographic script, to which the Greek Clemens Alexandrinus (died after 210 A.D.) already referred as *hieroglyphics* ("sacred signs"), was chiefly the script used on the monuments, but simpler, more cursive forms developed at a very early date for writing on papyrus. These simplified forms more or less lost their pictorial character and became similar to our letters. We call this book script *hieratic writing* (cf. Fig. 1). A

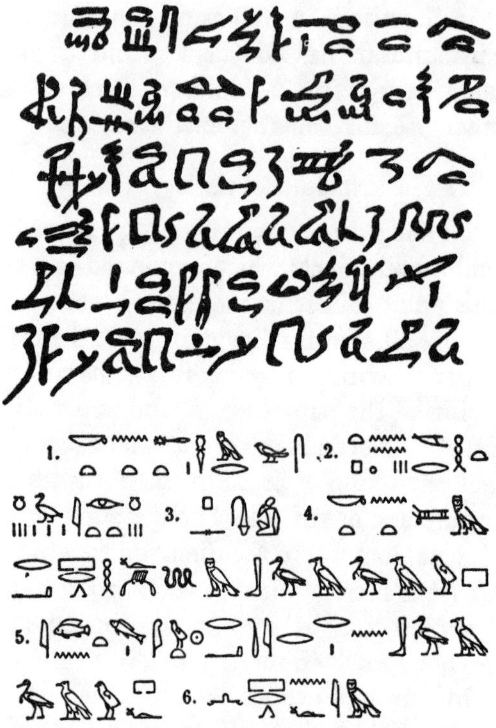

(1) k.t n.t ẖ.t mr.ś (2) tpnn mrḥ.t sꜣ.w jrt.t (3) ps swr (4) k.t n.t tm rdj pr ḥfꜣw m bꜣbꜣw (5) jnr.t šw.t rdj.tj r rꜣ n bꜣbꜣw.f (6) n pr.n.f jm

(1) Another (prescription) for the stomach when it is sick: (2) Cumin, goose fat, milk. (3) Cook, drink. (4) Another, in order not to permit that a snake come out of the hole: (5) A dry fish laid on the opening of its hole, (6) (then) it will not come out.

Fig. 1. Hieratic writing of the Papyrus Ebers with transposition into hieroglyphics. (From Erman, *Die Hieroglyphen*, pp. 37 and 76.)

further cursivification of the hieratic characters in the early part of the first millennium B.C. resulted in the development of the *demotic script* which resembles our shorthand and is very difficult to read (Fig. 2). These types of writing will be mentioned again on p. 16. All the three varieties of script are alike as to their inner principle, and therefore it will be sufficient to base the following discussion of the inner structure of Egyptian writing on the plastic hieroglyphic forms, made particularly impressive by their pictographic appearance. One more thing that I wish, however, to emphasize is that the following analysis of the Egyptian writing is a modern construction and has no footing in Egyptian antiquity.

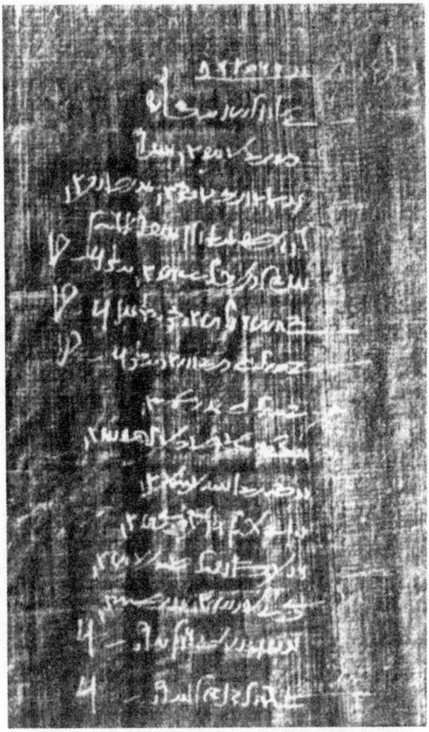

FIG. 2. Demotic Writing. (From Jensen, *Die Schrift*, Fig. 46.)

The Egyptian writing was not an alphabetic script, such as the one which we are accustomed by daily use to regard as something of a matter of course and naturally given. It consists of three distinct kinds of signs which impress us partly as strange, viz.: *word-signs, phonetic signs,* and *determinatives.* The word-signs, or *ideograms,* are signs which represent the *concept* of the living being or inanimate object illustrated and otherwise perceptible by the physical senses, i.e., concrete, and they represent that concept regardless of the spoken form. The Chinese ideographic script is composed almost exclusively of such signs, and they abound in the Egyptian script, too. (A few examples are shown in Fig. 3.) A script composed solely of pictographic word-signs

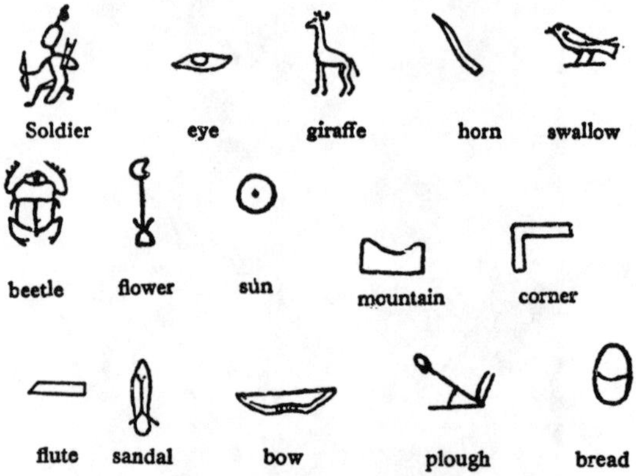

FIG. 3. Egyptian word-signs for living beings and concrete objects (according to Jensen).

would be understood, if need be, also by a person ignorant of the language, because it would represent only the underlying concepts behind the words, and not their spoken sound. Besides objects and beings directly perceptible by the physical senses, there are also sensorily perceptible acts, i.e., concepts expressed by *verbs.* It was possible to use simple word-signs, without phonetic references, for such concepts, too (Fig. 4). Furthermore, sensorily not perceptible concepts and actions,

FIG. 4. Egyptian word-signs for sensorily perceptible actions (according to Jensen).

i.e., nouns and verbs, could be expressed by some descriptive picture (Fig. 5). In order to write "south," they drew the picture of a lily, the flower characteristic of Upper Egypt;

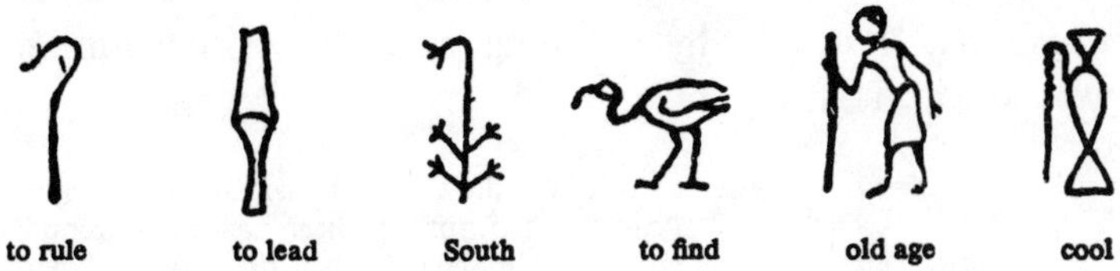

FIG. 5. Pictograms of sensorily not perceptible concepts and actions (according to Jensen and Erman).

"age" was indicated by a humped old man leaning on a staff, "cool" by a vessel with water running out of it, "to rule" by a sceptre, "to lead" by a commander's baton, "to go" by a pair of walking feet, "to fly" by a bird with its wings spread wide, "to eat" or "to speak" by a man who raises a hand to his mouth, etc. In these cases also, the pictogram expressed only the concept behind the word, but not its spoken sound.

But that spoken sound was frequently a very important factor. For this reason, it occurred to the Egyptians very early, probably way back in the initial stage of the development of the art of writing, that a concept difficult to represent pictorially could be symbolized by the picture of some*thing phonetically quite similar, but conceptually unrelated.* This was as if we wanted to represent, say, the concept underlying the verb *beat* by the picture of a *bit*, or the concept *bad* by the picture of a *bed*, or *hate* by drawing a *hat*. I have chosen these examples deliberately so as to make each example contain two words which are not completely identical, because the Egyptians also did not strive for any great accuracy. They drew the picture of a *swallow* (*wr*) to indicate *wr*, "*great*"; a *house* (*pr*) to indicate *prj*, "*to go out*"; a *beetle* (*ḫpr*) to indicate *ḫpr*, "*to become*"; a *frond* (*mś*) to indicate *mśj*, "*to give birth*"; a *basket*, *ḏr*, to indicate *ḏr*, "*boundary*"; etc. (Fig. 6a.) In fact, they could express *mśḏr*, "ear," either by the actual picture of an ear alone, or by the juxtaposition of the signs for *mś*, "*frond*," and *ḏr*, "*basket*," neither of which has conceptually anything whatsoever in common with an ear. (Cf. Fig. 6b.)

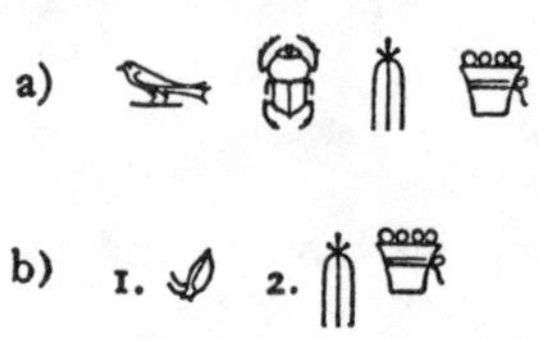

a) *wr*, "swallow" and *wr*, "great"; *ḫpr*, "beetle," and *ḫpr*, "to become"; *mś*, "frond," and *mśj*, "to give birth"; *ḏr*, "basket," and *ḏr*, "boundary."
b) *mśḏr*, "ear": 1. Pictogram. 2. *mś*, "frond" *ḏr*, "basket."

FIG. 6. Phonetic substitution by words of similar sound (according to Erman).

As indicated by my vowelless rendition of the Egyptian words, the Egyptians apparently attached little importance to vowels. At any rate, they did not represent them in their script. This fact is evident from the words known to us both in Old Egyptian and in Coptic, the language of the Christian Egyptians which is written with the Greek alphabet. E.g.,  *pḥ* "end" (*pahu* in Coptic), stands also for *pḥ*, "to attain" (*pōh* in Coptic), and *pḥtj*, "fame" (*pahte* in Coptic).

Phonetically considered, the signs used as phonetic symbols of words or parts of words are very different in size. Thus, *ḫpr*, "to become," and *śpr*, "to attain," contain three consonants each, whereas *wr*, "great," and *pḥ*, "to attain," contain only two. (See also Fig. 7 for several especially frequent bi-consonantal signs.) In most instances, we are ignorant of the exact number and positions of the vowels to be interpolated between the consonants, but in any case, some of these phonetic compounds seem to comprise only one syllable,

FIG. 7. Bi-consonantal phonetic signs. (According to Erman.)

others seem to consist of several syllables. It is a fact of particular importance that a few especially short words contained only one consonant (cf. Fig. 8). Since we are not aware of the vowels to be pronounced with these consonants, these signs impress us as characters of a *purely consonantal alphabet*. But they were by no means necessarily such to an Egyptian, because the consonant, which has been drilled into our consciousness by school education until we have come to regard it as something naturally given, is by no means regarded as such by primitive man. It was only in the Greek-Roman era that, through an acquaintance with European

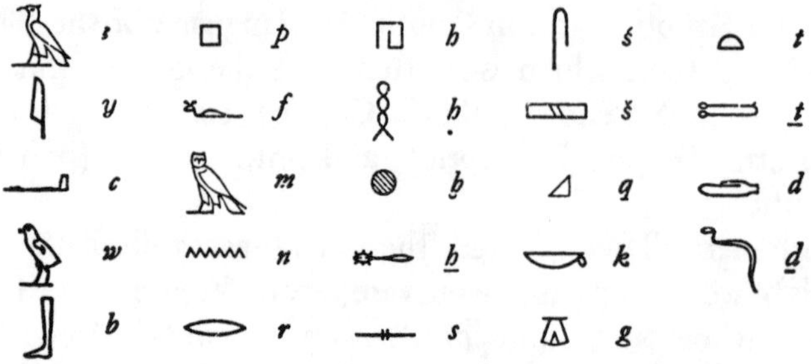

FIG. 8. List of the monoconsonantal signs of the Egyptian writing, the so-called "alphabet." (According to Erman.)

scripts, a sort of alphabet was developed which served primarily for writing Greek and Roman names, and therefore also took into consideration the vowels, to a certain extent.

But the ancient Egyptians never thought of dissecting their words into syllables, let alone into letters, and of eventually abandoning their word-signs and cumbersome syllabic symbols in order to write with pure monoconsonantal characters. Such a reform would have had also the result that all those words which differed only in the vowel within them would have been represented by the same written form, and ambiguities would have occurred in the written texts. (Just think of writing the English words *stake*, *stick*, *stock* and *stuck* by the consonants *stk* alone, the words *wand*, *wind* and *wound* simply by *wnd*, the words *scare*, *score*, *scour* and *scurry* simply by *scr!*) A strong strain of conservatism was another factor that kept the Egyptians from discontinuing the use of the pictogram of a word once it had been adopted.

In fact, they added phonetic signs also to word-signs which expressed words sufficiently by themselves. Thus, *śḏm*, "to hear," was expressed with sufficient clarity by , the picture of an ear, but they nevertheless added the picture of an owl, denoting *m*, to it, making it 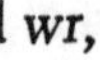. The word *wr*, "great," was represented clearly by , the picture of a swallow, and yet the Egyptians liked to append the picture of a mouth, , representing an *r*, i.e.: . This was how the many pleonastic written symbols of the Egyptians came into existence. They never did get rid of this complicated mixture of different signs, in fact there were times when they just could not pile up enough pleonastic symbols to satisfy them.

But even this complicated mixed method of writing was still not enough to make the vowelless Egyptian script unambiguous. How were the Egyptians to distinguish, e.g., *jb*, "kid," from *jbj*, "to be thirsty," when both words were written solely by the consonant signs *j* and *b*? In order to solve this problem, they resorted to the expedient of appending the picture of a kid when they wanted to write *jb*, and the picture of a man raising his hand to his mouth when they intended to denote *jbj*. (Fig. 9*a*.) The sign of a house could mean both *pr*, "house," and *prj*, "to go out"; when a pair of walking feet was added, it was expressed clearly that *prj*, "to go out," was meant. (Fig. 9*b*.)

The appending of these unpronounced signs to the word-signs provided a convenient means of graphically distin-

FIG. 9. Different concepts pronounced alike:
a) *jb*, "kid," and *jbj*, "to be thirsty."
b) *pr*, "house," and *prj*, "to go out."
(According to Erman.)

guishing words which would have otherwise been written alike. We call these mute explanatory signs *determinatives*. They constitute the previously mentioned third type of Egyptian written symbols and play a very important part. Such a determinative was appended to most Egyptian word-signs, with relatively few exceptions. Several of the most important determinatives are shown in Fig. 10. There is the drawing of a seated man which was added to names or designations of men. You see also the drawing of a woman, which appeared after names or designations of women. You see the

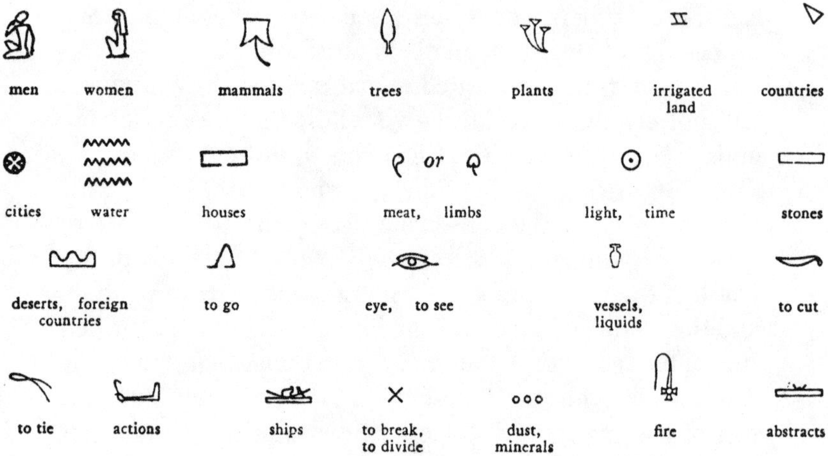

FIG. 10. Egyptian determinatives (according to Jensen).

determinatives for mammals (picture of a pelt with tail), trees, plants, irrigated land (drawing of a ditch), countries (demarcated stretch of land), cities (ground-plan of a walled city, with two streets crossing each other), water (three wavy lines), houses (ground-plan of a house with a door), meat (a piece of meat), time (picture of the disk of the sun), stones, lands (three mountains), to go, to see, liquids (vessel), to cut (knife), to tie (string), actions (beating arm), ships, to divide, minerals (grains), fire (coal basin with rope or chain for carrying it), and abstracts, i.e., spiritual things (book roll).

Only this system of three different classes of written signs (word-signs, phonetic symbols of varying coverage, and suffixed but unpronounced determinatives), confusing as it may appear to the uninitiated at first, did enable the Egyptians to express their language in writing with satisfactory unambiguity. The combined use of the different kinds of symbols is illustrated further by the few sentences shown in Fig. 11. The failure of the Egyptians to adopt changes in

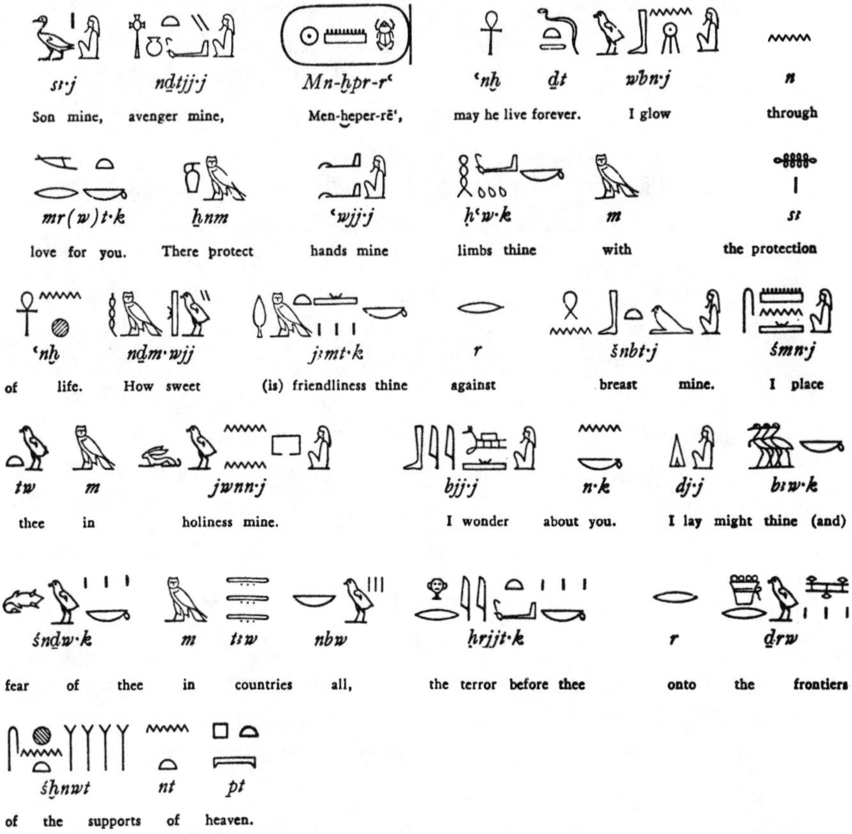

FIG. 11. Egyptian sentences (according to Jensen).

this method of writing, which strikes us as so very complicated, was due not solely to their conservative nature, but also to the very concrete motive that their writing would have been ambiguous and misleading without these complicated elements. The same consideration has frustrated all attempts in modern China and Japan at replacing the complicated ideographic and syllabic script by the Latin alphabetic writing.

The Egyptian script changed in its external form only. We have already mentioned the simplification of the pictographic monumental writing into the hieratic book script, and the further cursivification of the latter to the shorthand-like demotic form. Fig. 1 (p. 6) shows a few lines from the famous Papyrus Ebers, a hieratic medical book dating from 1600 B.C., now kept in the library of the Leipzig University; below the lines in hieratic script, you see the transcription of the signs into their hieroglyphic forms, followed by their transliteration in Latin characters and by their translation to English. In this connection, note that in the hieratic version the characters run, as in the original, from right to left, but the signs in the hieroglyphic transcription are printed in the left-to-right sequence to which we are accustomed in our own books. The direction of the demotic writing is shown in Fig. 2.

(c) *The Decipherment of the Egyptian Writing*

My readers may have grown impatient while following my presentation of our current knowledge of the Egyptian writing as seen *after* its decipherment, and now they are probably looking forward to an account of the process of the decipherment itself. But I had to approach the subject by such a roundabout way, for otherwise I would have been unable to describe the decipherment with the necessary clarity, and furthermore, now I can afford to be so much briefer about many a point.

People of antiquity did not rack their brains at all about a decipherment of the Egyptian script, the appearance of which was not unknown to them, because they had no interest in such things, and because they had the preconceived opinion that the hieroglyphics were no writing like all other writings, but concealed the secret wisdom of the philosopher priests, to be understood only by one likewise initiated into magico-mystic wisdom. This view was advanced, in late antiquity, by Horapollon, in his Greek book, *Hieroglyphica*, a book that remained unchallenged for centuries. Thus, a veritable ban still lay on the hieroglyphics even in the early part of the modern age, and even their first great decipherer, Champollion, was unable to shake off its hold for many years. This was also the reason why, in the 17th century, Athanasius Kircher, in his *Sphinx mystagogica*, could permit his imagination to run unchecked and interpret the simple phrase 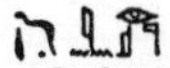 *ḏd-jn Wsjr*, "Osiris says," as "The life of things, after the defeat of Typhon, the moisture of Nature, through the vigilance of Anubis." Of course, more serious scientists rejected such absurdities and considered the secret of the hieroglyphics unsolvable. Thus the German-Danish archaeologist Zoega was unable to combat this skepticism in the late 18th century, although he regarded the hieroglyphics soberly and correctly recognized the fact that the names of the Egyptian monarchs were surrounded by an oval ring, which today we call a *cartouche*. (Cf. Fig. 13.)

The interest in the civilization and language of Egypt then was enhanced unexpectedly by the historical events. One of the original aims of Napoleon's daring Egyptian campaign, parallel with the main political purposes of that undertaking, was to conduct an archaeological study of the land. Only then did the people of the West learn how many relics of Egyptian antiquity still lay preserved under the sands of the Egyptian desert. And it so happened just then that the soil of Egypt presented scientific research with the best means to decipher the hieroglyphic inscriptions which were becoming available by the thousands; that means was a *bilinguis*, i.e., an inscription written in two languages, namely, in the unknown Egyptian tongue, and in the well known Greek language of Alexander's time. Strictly speaking, it was actually a *trilinguis*, a text written in three languages—in Early Egyptian, written in hieroglyphics, in Neo-Egyptian (demotic), in demotic characters, and in Greek, in Greek characters. It was found during the construction of entrenchments at Rosetta (in the Nile Delta) in 1799. However, the inscription was not intact; large sections were missing from the portion in Early Egyptian, chiefly at its beginning, and so were several words at the beginning of the first lines of the demotic portion, and the final words of the last lines of the Greek portion. (Cf. Fig. 12.) The Greek text was nevertheless almost completely understandable. It contained a resolution of the Egyptian priests in honor of the young monarch Ptolemy Epiphanes upon his ascension to the throne on March 27, 196 B.C. He had done so much good for the temples and their priests that the priesthood decided to honor him as a god and to erect a statue honoring him in every temple, with an inscription identical with this one.

Naturally, the report of this find aroused tremendous interest and rekindled the hope that the secret of the hieroglyphics would be solved at last. But it was found soon that things were not as simple as all that. The almost completely intact demotic portion seemed to be more suitable for the undertaking than the seriously damaged hieroglyphic text. Although a few frequently recurring names in the Greek part could be identified with certain groups of signs recurring with equal frequency in the demotic part (thus, in 1802, the

FIG. 12. The Rosetta Stone. (From Sethe, *Vom Bilde zum Buchstaben*, Table II.)

Swede Akerblad determined that the group of demotic characters reproduced in our Fig. 13 was the equivalent of the

FIG. 13. The name of Ptolemy in demotic and hieroglyphic characters. (From Erman, *Die Hieroglyphen*, p. 7.)

name "Ptolemy"), this cursive script with its many interfused symbols (ligatures) contained so many unclarities that no real progress was achieved. Nobody even dared tackle the seriously damaged hieroglyphic text at first, especially since hieroglyphics still were being regarded as secret symbols.

Thomas Young (1773–1829), the English physicist who earned fame by his wave theory of light, was the first man to dare attempt the decipherment of the hieroglyphic text, too, and he identified the name of Ptolemy also in that portion, within the cartouche already discovered by Zoega. (Cf. Fig. 13.) His reasoning that at least the Greek names of persons could not have possessed that character of secret symbols which was still ascribed to hieroglyphics in general, led him to dissect this group, as shown in Fig. 14. He interpreted another inscription as the name of Berenyce (cf. Fig. 15a),

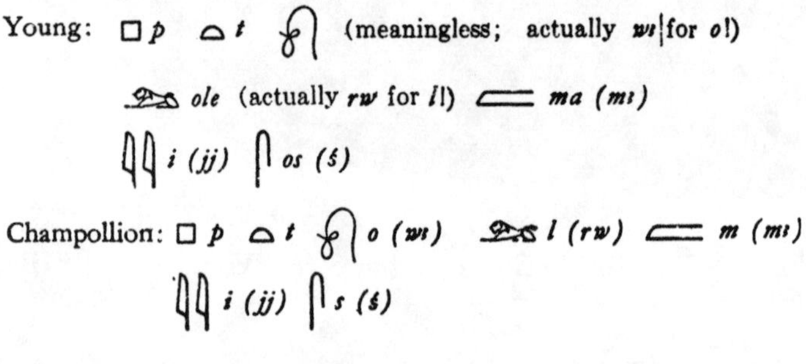

FIG. 14. Analysis of the name "Ptolemy," according to Young and Champollion.

which helped in the identification of a few more letters. In an article published in the Encyclopaedia Britannica in 1819, he tried to identify also the equivalents of individual Greek words in the hieroglyphic portion. But attempts at decipherment were still hampered by the belief in the symbolic nature of the hieroglyphics.

The man who was the first to succeed in actually deciphering the hieroglyphics was the young Frenchman Jean François Champollion (1790–1832) who, uncommonly gifted

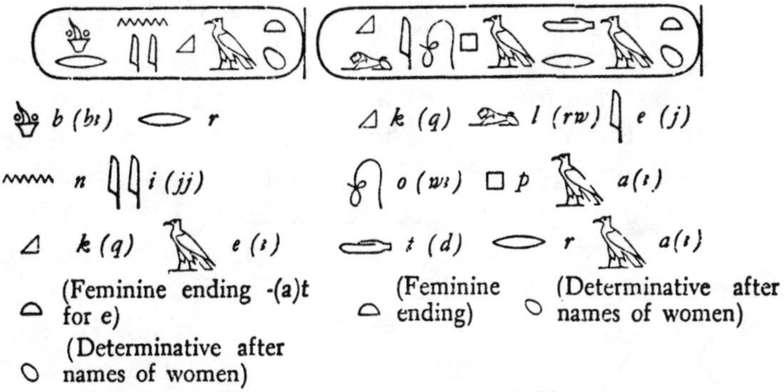

a) Berenyce b) Cleopatra

FIG. 15. The names *Berenyce* and *Cleopatra*, and their analysis. (According to Jensen.)

and mature at a very early age and raised as a prodigy, determined as a mere boy of eleven to become the decipherer of the hieroglyphics. But he too was unable to rid himself, for many long years, of the belief in a symbolism of those signs. But he prepared himself for his chosen life task by careful study. First of all, he learned Coptic, the language of the Christian Egyptians which is written in Greek characters, and which—as we know today—is quite unsuitable as a bridge to an understanding of the ancient tongue both because of its quite impoverished vocabulary and its strongly changed grammatical structure. Then he obtained reproductions of every accessible Egyptian inscription and papyrus, and at a cost of fifteen years of extremely tedious work, he compiled from them all the forms of the hieroglyphic signs, with their graphically simplified hieratic and demotic equivalents—but he did all this without yet daring proceed to the reading of one single character.

An important achievement was, in 1813, his reasoning that the ancient Egyptian language, like Coptic, must have expressed the personal pronouns in certain cases by the endings *-i* for *I*, *-k* for *thou* (masculine), *-f* for *he*, *-s* for *she*, -n for *we*, ***-tən*** for ye, and -u for *they*. And he was able to ascertain at least that the hieroglyphic 𓆑 corresponded to the Greek words meaning *he* and *him* in the Greek portion of the Rosetta Stone. His studies of the history of writing enabled him then to recognize at once that the Coptic letter ϥ *f* (as well as some other Coptic characters) was actually that very hieroglyphic 𓆑 *f*. But he was still burdened with the belief in the symbolic nature of the hieroglyphics. He still thought that in the hieroglyphic version of the name of Ptolemy, known since Young, the likeness of the lion, 𓃭 (*rw* = *l*), was to be regarded as a symbol of war—p(t)*olemos* in Greek—hidden within the name of Ptolemy.

He did not abandon this erroneous belief until December 21, 1821. A simple count proved then that the still existing hieroglyphic text of the Rosetta Stone contained about three times as many signs as there were words in the Greek text. It was therefore quite unthinkable that each hieroglyphic represented a whole word, and the hieroglyphic inscription was sure to have contained a considerable number of phonetic symbols as well. And only after arriving at this conclusion did he apply to entire names the methods of research into the history of writing, formerly applied to individual symbols only; he converted the demotic equivalents of the Greek names appearing on the Rosetta Stone, character by character, into their hieratic and further into their hieroglyphic forms, and, for instance, when applying this procedure to the name of "Ptolemy," he actually arrived at the same hieroglyphic symbol group which appeared in the cartouche in the hieroglyphic portion of the Rosetta Stone (Fig. 13). So now he dared proceed to determine the meaning of each individual sign, as shown in Fig. 14. Analogously, going backward from the demotic form, he reconstructed the name "Cleopatra" as the series of signs shown in Fig. 15 (*b*), and the identical way of writing that name was actually found in an inscription written in hieroglyphics and in Greek, discovered in January 1822, so that now he had established the values of a few more signs.

The taboo was broken now, and Champollion identified other inscriptions as the Greek and Latin names *Alexandros, Autokrator, Tiberius, Domitianus, Germanicus, Traianus,* etc. (Fig. 16). But he still held the belief that only foreign, non-Egyptian names could be written this way. Only on

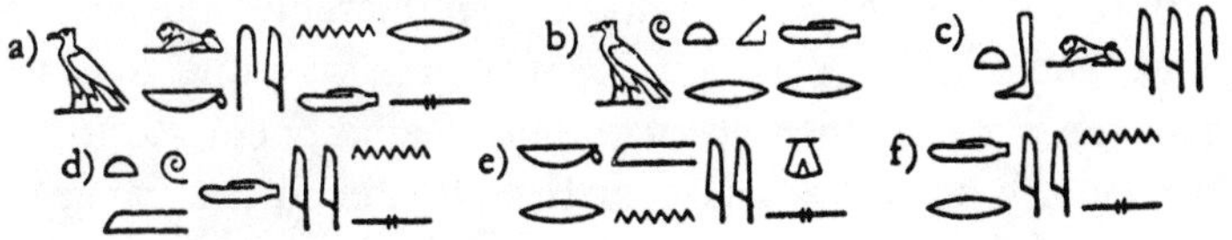

FIG. 16. The names *Alexandros* (a), *Autokrator* (b), *Tiberius* (c), *Domitianus* (d), *Germanicus* (e) and *Traianus* (f) in hieroglyphic script (according to Erman).

September 14, 1822, when he immediately recognized in certain new hieroglyphic inscriptions the names of the ancient Egyptian rulers *Re-mss* (*Rʿ-mśś*), i.e., *Ramses,* and *Thout-ms* (*Dḥwtj-mś*), i.e., *Thutmosis* (Fig. 17), did it finally become clear to him that the ancient script also had

FIG. 17. The names *Ramses* (a) and *Thutmosis* (b) in hieroglyphic script. (From Erman, *Die Hieroglyphen*, p. 11.)

used no mystic symbols, but phonetic characters, and that his laborious research had re-discovered not merely the way of writing Greek and Roman names in Egyptian characters, but the ancient writing itself. On September 27, 1822, he was able to notify the Academy of Paris, in his famous *Lettre à M. Dacier relative à l'alphabet des hiéroglyphes phonétiques,** that he had succeeded in deciphering the Egyptian hieroglyphics.

In the further decipherment, Champollion enjoyed the benefit of the enormous preliminary work which he had done by comparing the individual signs through so many years. In 1825, he was already able to translate an Early Egyptian inscription of Amenophis III. Further hieroglyphic inscriptions and hieratic papyri came next. He was able to learn also the correct meaning of the great epic poem glorifying the victory of Ramses II over the Hittites in the battle of Kadesh (cf. p. 4). Let it be emphasized, however, in the words of Erman,** that "it was no well organized knowledge that he bequeathed to his successors at the time of his premature death (1832). He had ingeniously comprehended properly the words and sentences, but he never formulated a clear comprehension of the system of the script which he knew how to read." A *decipherer,* who skips over scruples and dif-

* "Letter to Mr. Dacier, concerning the alphabet of the phonetic hieroglyphics."

** *Die Hieroglyphen,* p. 12. (Sammlung Göschen, No. 608.)

ficulties ingeniously, and a *philologist*, who ponders his results carefully as he forges them into rules, are fundamentally different and *must not be mistaken for each other*. It should be, therefore, no surprise that Champollion's decipherment was by no means universally accepted at first. For three more decades, even scientists were not willing to admit anything more than the fact that at best a few royal names could be deciphered, but they insisted that everything else was pure fantasy. Only in 1866 did the discovery of another bilingual inscription, the lengthy *Decree of Canopus*, bring scientific confirmation of a whole series of facts which Champollion had ingeniously discovered.

The new infant science thus had to mature for several decades before it eventually built a scientifically guaranteed Egyptian philology on the foundation left by Champollion. The details of this development are, at best, of interest to the specialist, but certainly not to the general public. For this reason, I shall mention only a few more principal facts at this time.

The great and versatile German scientist Richard Lepsius was the one who ultimately clarified the Egyptian system of writing and, by his translation and analysis of the Decree of Canopus, silenced the doubts of serious scientists, too, as regards the decipherment. Next to him, mention is due to several more careful, sober savants, namely: the English Birch, the astute Irishman Hincks, whom we shall meet again when we shall review the decipherment of the cuneiform writing, and the French de Rougé. Birch and Hincks are to be credited first of all with the correct explanation of the determinatives. The German Heinrich Brugsch was a man of a more tempestuous character; he was still an undergraduate in 1848, when he cast further light on the intricate demotic script which Egyptologists are inclined to shun even today.

Among the personages of the subsequent period of philological development, a few brief words of praise are due to the French Chabas and Maspéro, and to the English Budge and Gardiner. The credit for the really solid lexical and grammatical foundations belongs above all to German research, and primarily to the strict "Berlin School" of Adolf Erman (1854–1937) whose thorough studies of writing habits enabled him to distinguish the individual linguistic periods and to establish the position of the Neo-Egyptian of the late second millennium B.C. as an independent language, ranking side by side with Early Egyptian. He steered lexical research and, above all, morphology—still hampered by lack of clarity as a result of the vowelless script—onto such firm tracks as the state of affairs permitted, and he was the man who formulated the now universally accepted view of Egyptian in phonological respects, too. Whereas some others, even in the twentieth century, still reckoned with the possibility that the Egyptian script partly indicated vowels, next to the consonants expressed, Erman consistently advocated the view of the purely consonantal nature of the Egyptian phonetic symbols. His school has remained authoritative in all linguistic investigations of Egyptian antiquity.

(d) *The Meroitic Script and Its Study*

The use of the Egyptian system of writing was limited chiefly to Egypt itself, above all because it was so closely tailored to the structure of the Egyptian language that it would have been difficult to adopt it to another tongue. There is, however, a script which can be recognized to be an offshoot of the Egyptian, viz., the script of the so-called "Ethiopian" empire of Meroë, situated to the south of Egypt, from the 1st century B.C. till the 3rd or 4th century A.D. As for the shapes of the characters, the Meroitic script looks totally like Egyptian writing, and it even developed two varieties analogously to the Egyptian script, namely: a monumental script of a pictographic (hieroglyphic) character, the symbols of which partly look like those of the Egyptian hieroglyphic script, and a cursive form (although it is found on monuments, too) which resembles the demotic writing of Egypt.

The striking feature of the Meroitic script is the small number of its characters; it consists of a mere 23 characters, in contrast to the hundreds of Egyptian symbols. This fact can be explained most easily by assuming that whereas the Meroitic script emulated the appearance of the Egyptian script more or less closely, it was essentially an *alphabetic script* (without word-signs, polyconsonantal signs and determinatives). One is all the more justified in thinking of the prototype of the Greek script because the Meroitic system seems to have used also vowel signs, although not consistently.

Meroitic inscriptions have been known since about 1820, but they were regarded as undecipherable and untranslatable for a long time, until the English Egyptologist Griffith succeeded, between 1910 and 1930, in deciphering them to a certain extent at least. He started out from the inscription of Benâgâ which is written on the whole in Egyptian, but with the names of the king and queen appearing both in Egyptian and in Meroitic. Using this inscription as a starting point, a more or less certain way of *reading* the symbols was established, whereas the *translation* of the unknown language of Meroë, not as yet demonstrable to be related to any known language, is still a very precarious matter. Fig. 18 shows the hieroglyphic and demotic alphabets of the Meroitic language, whereas Fig. 19 presents the reproduction of a demotic Meroitic inscription, with its transliteration and translation by Griffith.

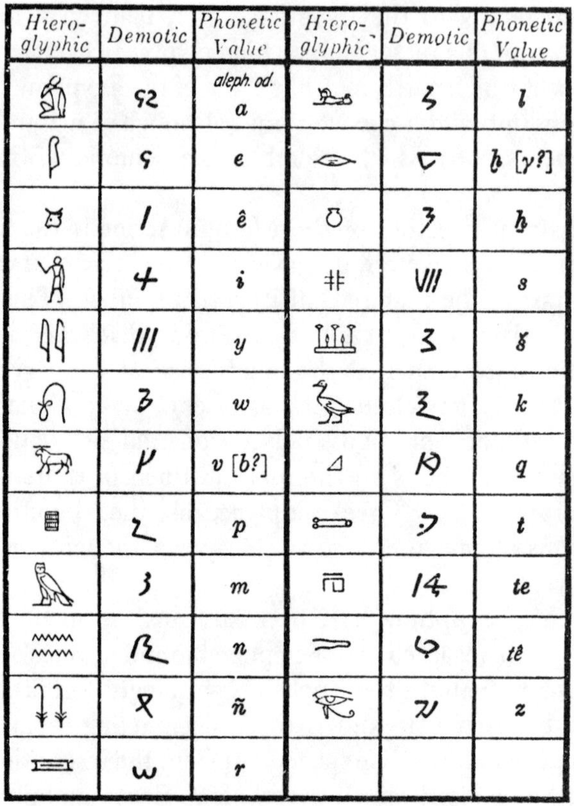
Hiero-glyphic
Demotic
Phonetic Value
aleph. od.
a
e
ê
i
y
w
v [b?]
p
m
n
ñ
r
l
ḫ [γ?]
ḫ
s
š
k
q
t
te
tê
z

FIG. 18. The Meroitic alphabets. (From Jensen, *Die Schrift*, Fig. 49.)

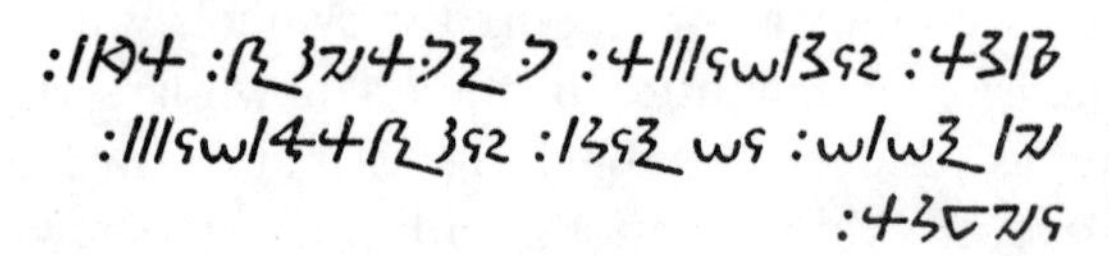

: *wêši* : *ašêreyi* : *tktiz-mn* : *iqê* : *zêkrêr* : *erkelê* : *amnitêrey* : *ezḫli*

"Isis (and) Osiris, protect Taktiz-Amon, (the one) begotten (by) Zekarer, born (by) Amon-tares"

2. Cuneiform Writing

The cuneiform writing of the Near East is far less well known to the general public than are the hieroglyphics of Egypt. Even the people of antiquity no longer had any accurate notion of it, only very ancient Greece had known it as *Assyria grammata*, "Assyrian letters." The people of the modern era found it more difficult to get used to this harsh jumble of wedges, remotely reminiscent of the Chinese writing, than to the neat pictographic shapes of the old Egyptian script. But the ancient Orient found the cuneiform characters to be by far the more important and practical system of writing, and their use spread far beyond the boundaries of Babylon, their birthplace, and they were employed for writing numerous other Near Eastern languages. Let us, however, confine our consideration to the native land of the cuneiform script and contemplate Babylonia and Assyria somewhat more closely.

(a) *Land and People, History and Civilization of Mesopotamia*

Like the civilization in Egypt, the oldest civilization in the Near East also sprouted forth along rivers, in Mesopotamia, between the Euphrates and Tigris rivers which in those days still flowed separately into the Persian Gulf. These two rivers gave the country its name, for *Mesopotamia* is Greek for "the land between the rivers." In Mesopotamia, however, the arable land was not confined so completely to the strips along the rivers, although the alluvial land, criss-crossed by the many canals of the Euphrates, does constitute the major part of it.

The oldest identifiable inhabitants of the land were the *Sumerians*, an ancient civilized race of undetermined origin. But from the early part of the third millennium B.C. on, they shared the land with the Semitic *Babylonians* who had immigrated, as a race of nomads, from the Syrian desert, as did also the *Amorites* about 2000 B.C., the Aramaeans about 1000 B.C., and the Arabs in the Christian era.

The political development of the populace was no less disuniform than its origin. Insofar as we can see, the Sumerians seem to have inhabited the land since time immemorial; at any rate, the English excavations in Ur and the German ones in Uruk, which unearthed relics of very ancient times, predating even the development of any writing at all, failed to disclose any indication of any older race. For a long time there was no unified government in Mesopotamia. Sumeria was a land of many small, independent city states to which the designation "Sumeria" is applicable in the racial sense only. From about 2500 B.C. on, there was a Semitic population next to the Sumerians, in Akkadia, to the north of Sumeria, wherefore most recently the designation *Akkadians* has been adopted and used parallelly with the reference to "Babylonians," and we speak now also of an *Akkadian*, i.e., Babylonian-Assyrian language. One of the mightiest rulers of early Babylonia was Sargon I (about 2350–2300 B.C.) whom later ages regarded as the archetype of great monarchs (as did other nations regard Alexander the Great or Charlemagne). At the end of the third millennium B.C., the Sumerians enjoyed another period of second bloom under Gudea of Lagash (about 2050 B.C.?) who united most of the land for the first time, but the united realm disintegrated again into small states later, during the struggle against mighty Elam in the east.

The unification of all of Babylonia was finally accomplished by Hammurabi of Babylon, an Akkadianized Amorite, the most brilliant monarch in Babylonian history, who made decisive the victory of the Semitic race over the Sumerians. The exact period when Hammurabi had lived remained undecided for a long time; the earlier authorities hesitated for a long time between 2100 (or even 2300) and about 1900 B.C., and only quite recently was it decided with finality that Hammurabi had lived from 1728 to 1686 B.C., a contemporary of the Assyrian king Šamši-Adad I who is definitely known to have lived 1749–1717 B.C. From then on there was a unified Semitic empire in Mesopotamia, in which the Sumerians were gradually absorbed. Hammurabi instituted great administrative reforms, recorded in his famous Code which was discovered by the French in Susa in 1903. Babylon became the capital of the realm known to us from that era on as Babylonia. Marduk, the youthful city god of Babylon, became the national deity, and the classical Babylonian language was used as the daily vernacular of the empire.

The empire of Hammurabi did not last long; the alien Kassites (or Cossaeans) subdued Babylonia and ruled it for a long time. But their rule (about 1600–1200 B.C.) was gentle and peaceful. In the meantime, Assyria, in the north of the land on the Tigris, flourished and prospered ever more and more. Assur, a Babylonian city state, is known to have existed even in a much earlier era, and it had gone through alternate stages of political might and decline. In the 15th century B.C., it was a tributary of Mitanni, the mighty Hurrian empire of northwestern Mesopotamia, but after the collapse of the latter it became independent and kept gaining in importance. Salmanassar I dealt a final death blow to Ḫanigalbat, the successor of Mitanni, about 1270 B.C. Tukulti-Ninurta I laid siege to Babylon about 1230 B.C., and Tiglath-Pileser I was the first ruler of the Near East to push forward as far as the Mediterranean, about 1100 B.C.

From then on, Assyria was constantly ruled by a drive westward which is reflected in the Old Testament, too. Let us mention here the following outstanding personages among the rulers of the Neo-Assyrian empire: Salmanassar

III (858–824 B.C.) who fought against Damascus, Tyre and Sidon, and also against Yehu of Israel; Tiglath-Pileser III (745–727 B.C.) who supported Aḥaz of Judah against Pekah of Israel, and whose mastery Hoseah of Israel eventually had to acknowledge; Sargon II (721–705 B.C.), victor over mighty Urarṭu, conqueror of Samaria, who took the ten northern tribes of Israel into captivity; Sennacherib (704–681 B.C.) who made Nineveh his capital and laid an unsuccessful siege to Jerusalem; Assarhaddon (680–669 B.C.) who even conquered Egypt for a short while and thus brought the Assyrian empire to its largest geographical expansion; and finally, Assurbanipal (668–626 B.C.), destroyer of the Elamite empire, but better known for his literary interests and his library in Nineveh.

The Indo-European Medes of Iran joined forces with the Babylonians in 606 B.C., and they succeeded in overthrowing and destroying the Assyrian empire. That victory made the Babylonians arise once again, after the long oppression by Assyria, and enjoy a brief second bloom of the Neo-Babylonian empire, among whose rulers mention is due above all to Nebuchadnezzar II (604–562 B.C.), destroyer of Jerusalem in 586 B.C., who took the Jews into Babylonian captivity. The Persian Cyrus defeated the Babylonian army and ended the independence of the country in 539 B.C. Babylonia remained a province, first of the Persian empire, then of Alexander the Great and his successors, later of Rome and still later of the Parthian empire, until the Arabs finally made Bagdad the successor of Babylon.

Nor is it possible to say here more than just a few words about the civilization of the Sumerians, Babylonians and Assyrians. The reader is referred to Meissner's comprehensive *Babylonien und Assyrien** where he will find detailed information on the Sumerian-Babylonian religion with its

* 2 vols., Heidelberg. 1920, 1925.

ancient divine triad, Anu (god of the heavens), Enlil (god of the air and the earth) and Ea (god of the subterranean watery depths), with the goddess Maḫ or Ninḫursag, "Queen of the Gods," as well as the younger triad, Sin (moon god), Shamash (sun god) and Adad (weather god), with the goddess Ishtar. As Babylon was becoming more powerful, also its own city god, Marduk, gained an important position in the pantheon, as did also Assur, the god of Assyria, when the power of the latter was on the ascent. Mesopotamia developed a rich mythology and produced a series of epic poems; let it suffice to mention here merely the Creation Epic, in praise of Marduk, and the great Gilgamesh Epic, the deluge episode of which attracted such great attention because of the extent to which it agrees with the Biblical report of the Flood. Babylonian architecture did not produce quite such impressive creations as those of Egypt, because it worked with a perishable material, clay brick, but the Ishtar Gate of Babylon (reconstructed in the Berlin Museum) is nevertheless admirable, and so is the plastic art of the Neo-Assyrian period for its artistic perfection and true-to-nature details. Among the sciences of Babylonia, mention is due above all to mathematics and also to astronomy, jointly with astrology, which exerted a strong influence on the West and gave us also the system of dividing time into weeks. The study of the history of Babylonian-Assyrian law is an important branch of the study of the Ancient Orient, because of the great codes of laws, among which the Babylonian Code of Hammurabi and the still older Code of King Bilalama of Ešnunna (about 1884–1863 B.C.) as well as the Middle-Assyrian Book of Laws are the most outstanding, and also because of the many thousands of private documents, originating from various regions of the Near East, which illustrate the living application of the system of laws.

(b) *The Essential Features of the Cuneiform Writing*

Of the many cultural achievements of Mesopotamia, its script and system of writing are those which are of interest to us here. A cursory look seems to reveal a profound difference between this script and the Egyptian writing. Egypt used paper for writing material, for its literary records at least, whereas Babylonia used clay tablets. The characters were scratched into the soft clay with a wooden stylus, and the tablet was then fired to make it durable. Odd and inconvenient as this writing material may appear to us, the use of the clay tablet spread out from Babylonia, together with the cuneiform writing, and was adopted in remote parts of the Near East, in Syria and in Asia Minor; in fact, the clay tablet was used also for writing the Cretan-Minoan script and language in Crete and in prehistoric Greece.

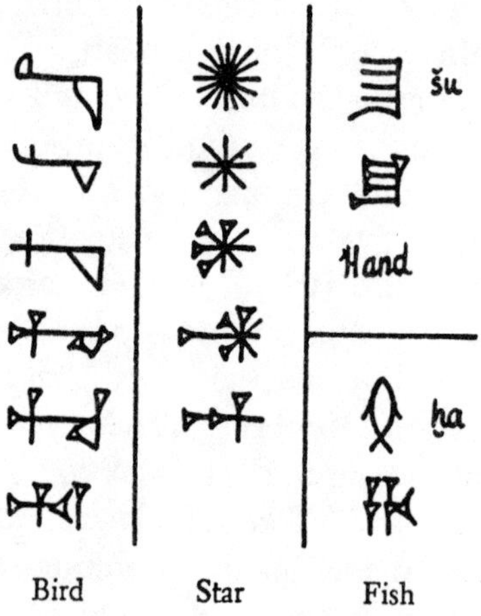

FIG. 20. Old Sumerian pictograms and their development into cuneiform symbols. (Friedrich, *Archiv Orientálni*, Vol. 19, Table XI.)

Also the characters of the Babylonian-Assyrian script appear to be basically different from the Egyptian symbols. The Egyptian writing originally employed clear, plastic, impressive pictograms which, however, later became simplified in daily use; the Babylonian-Assyrian writing looks like a hodgepodge of confusing combinations of wedges which remind the uninitiated of the writing of China. But at least this difference is a secondary one: cuneiform writing also was invented by the Sumerians originally as a pictographic script, as demonstrated by a few examples in Fig. 20, and only the practice of writing them with a wooden stylus in soft clay made the individual pictograms degenerate very soon into wedge shapes, in which the old pictographic form can be detected in a few instances only. There are spatial and temporal differences within cuneiform writing as such, too, between the intricate Old Babylonian, Old Assyrian (Cappadocian), Middle Babylonian and Middle Assyrian cuneiform script, on the one hand, and the simpler Neo-Assyrian and Neo-Babylonian varieties on the other (see Figs. 21a, 21*b*, and 21c for specimens), but these differences will not impress the laymen as strongly as the differences between the hieroglyphic and the hieratic and, especially, the demotic scripts.

On the other hand, the Egyptian script and the cuneiform writing are very similar as to their *inner nature and principle*, because the same three kinds of signs which we have observed in the Egyptian system of writing are present also in the cuneiform script, viz.: *word-signs* or *ideograms, phonetic signs*, and *determinatives*. Also in the cuneiform writing many words *can* be expressed by individual word-signs which denote only the concept in question, irrespective of the spoken sound of the word; the spoken word may sound quite different in Sumerian and in Akkadian, in given cases also in Hittite, Hurrian, Urartaean or Elamite, but the written sym-

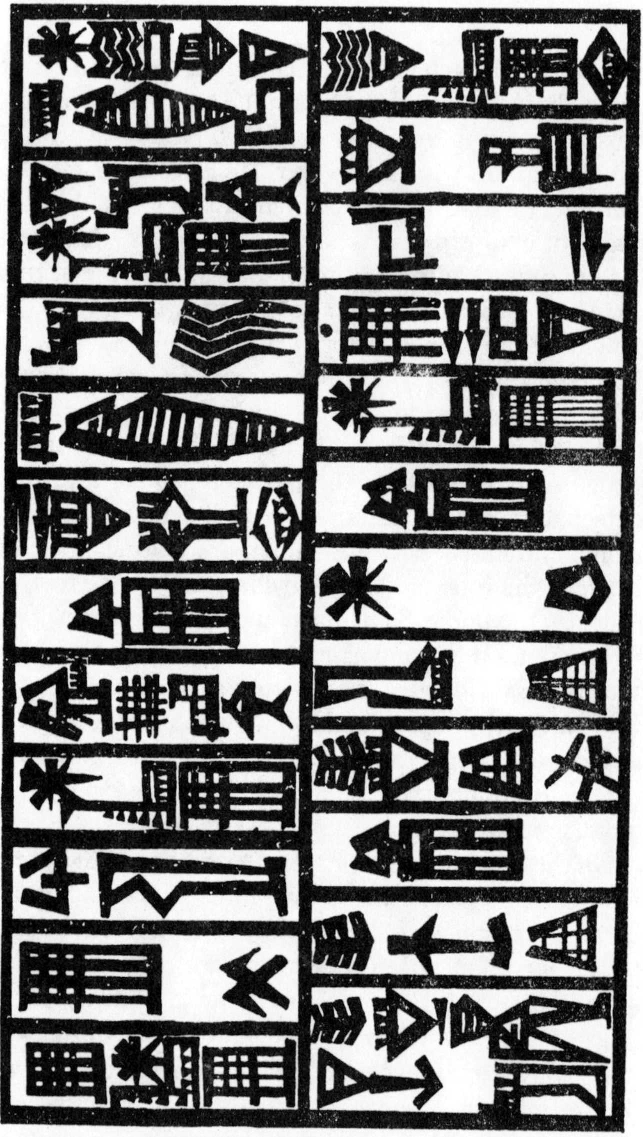

FIG. 21. Early and late forms of Babylonian cuneiform writing. (a) Old Akkadian inscription of King Šarganišaralim, with (b) transcription into Neo-Assyrian script (opposite page). (Böhl, *Akkadian Chrestomathy*, I, pp. 40–41.)

(1) ^{d}*Šar-ga-ni-šar-alim* (2) *mār Da-ti-* ^{d}*En-lil* (3) *da-núm* (4) *šar* (5) *A-ga-de*^{KI} (6) *ù* (7) *ba*$_{11}$*-ú-la-ti* (8) ^{d}*En-lil* (9) *bāni* (10) *E-kur* (11) *bīt* ^{d}*En-lil* (12) *in Nippurim*^{KI} (13) *ša tuppam* (14) *su*$_{4}$*-a* (15) *u-sa-za-ku-ni* (16) ^{d}*En-lil* (17 *ù* (18) ^{d}*Šamaš* (19) *išid-su* (20) *li-su-ḫa* (21) *ù* (22) *ēr-su* (23) *li-il-gu-da*

"Šarganišaralim, son of Dati-Enlil, the Mighty One, King of Akkad and of the domains of Enlil, (is) the builder of E-kur, the temple of Enlil, in Nippur. If anybody alters this document, may Enlil and Shamash tear out his foundation and sweep away his seed."

FIG. 21*b*

bol of the concept is identical in all these languages. Thus, e.g., 𒀭 (originally the picture of a star) was the ideogram for the concept "heaven" in every language written in cuneiform characters, and it was pronounced *an* in Sumerian, *šamû* in Akkadian, *nepiš* in Hittite, etc. But the same sign was also the ideogram for the concept "god," and when used in that sense, it was pronounced *dingir* in Sumerian, *ilu* in

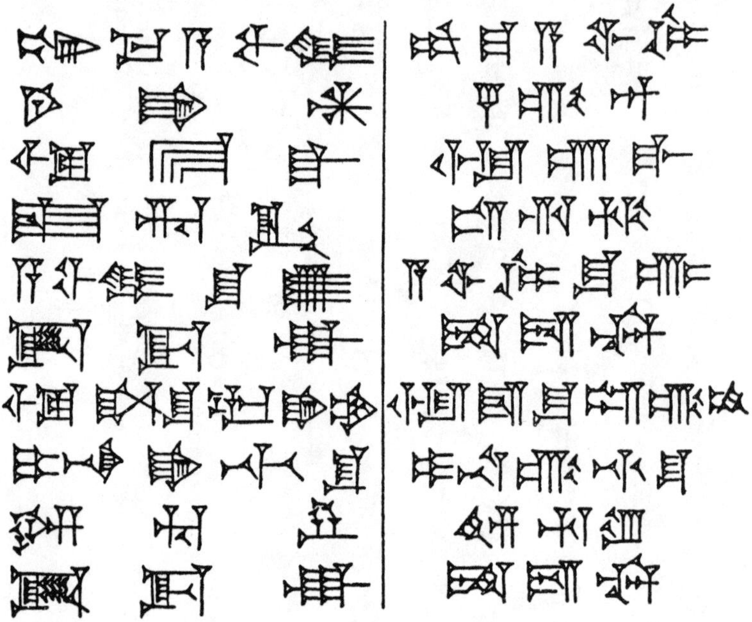

(31) *šum-ma a-we-lum* (32) *namkur ilim* (33) *ù ēkallim* (34) *iš-ri-iq* (35) *a-we-lum šu-ú* (36) *id-da-ak* (37) *ù ša šu-úr-ga-am* (38) *i-na ga-ti-šu* (39) *im-ḫu-ru* (40) *id-da-ak*

"If a citizen has stolen a possession of a god or of a temple, such citizen shall be killed. Also he who has accepted the stolen goods out of his hands, shall be killed."

FIG. 21c. Early and late forms of Babylonian cuneiform writing: (c) Early Babylonian script (Art. 6 of Hammurabi's Laws) with transcription in Neo-Assyrian writing.

Akkadian, *šiuni-* in Hittite, *eni-* in Hurrian, etc. The ideogram  meant "king" and was pronounced *lugal* in Sumerian, *šarru* in Akkadian, *ḫaššu-* in Hittite, *ivri-* in Hurrian, *ereli-* in Urartaean.

These words could be represented also by phonetic signs or by combinations of an ideographic symbol representing the stem of the word and phonetic signs for grammatical endings (Fig. 22). The noteworthy fact in this connection is that unlike the phonetic symbols of the Egyptian script, the cuneiform phonetic characters do not represent sometimes bigger and sometimes smaller consonant clusters without indicating any vowels, but stand for *clear-cut syllables, including vowels*. These syllables are, to use our classification

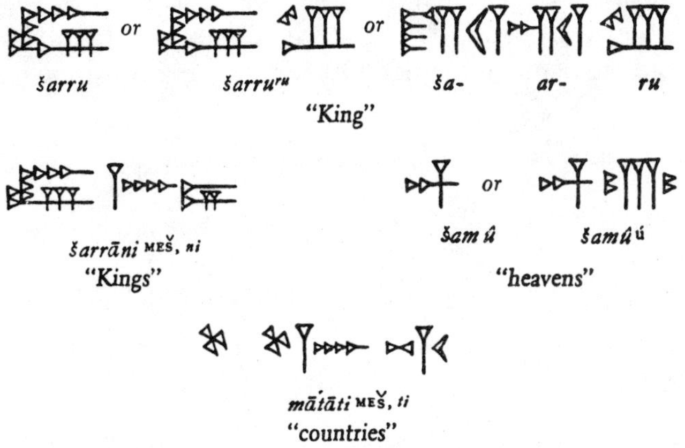

FIG. 22. Examples of mixed writing (word stem represented by ideograms, endings by phonetic characters).

of sounds, either consonant + vowel (e.g., *ba, mi, ru*) or vowel + consonant (e.g., *ad, ir, uk*) or finally (more rarely) consonant + vowel + consonant (e.g., *bar, kid, lum*) combinations. Each complex syllable of the last-mentioned type can be split into two simple ones, namely one of each of the other two types, because *bar* could be written also as *ba* + *ar*, *kid* as *ki* + *id*, *lum* as *lu* + *um*, etc. But let it be emphasized in particular that *a single, lone consonant can never be expressed in cuneiform script.*

The unpronounced *determinatives* play an especially important part in the cuneiform writing. They were mostly prefixed to the symbol of the word which they were intended to qualify, although in certain rarer cases they were placed after it. A specific determinative, consisting of a vertical wedge, appears before the names of male persons; another one, identical with the ideogram meaning "man," was prefixed to the designations of professions; a third one, originally the likeness of a vulva, appears before the names of women and designations of female occupations. The above mentioned ideogram for "god" appears as a determinative before the names of deities. Other determinatives were used

^{d}A-nu *^{d}En-lil* *^{d}É-a*

Fig. 23. The names of three gods with determinatives

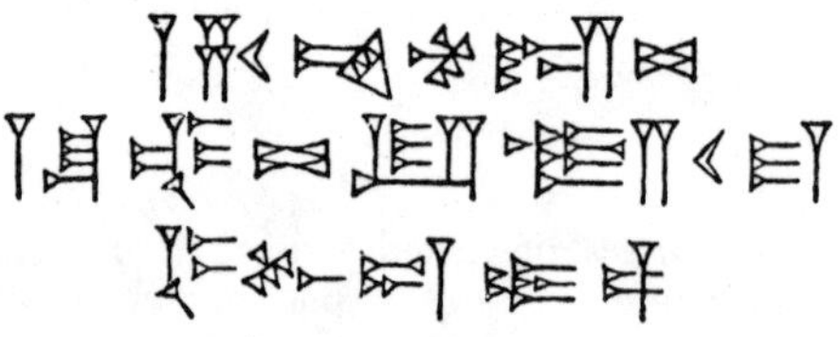

1. *^{I}Ḫa-am-mu-ra-bi*
2. *^{I}Šu-up-pi-lu-li-u-ma*
3. *^{F}Pu-du-ḫé-pa*

Fig. 24. Two names of men and a woman's name, with determinatives

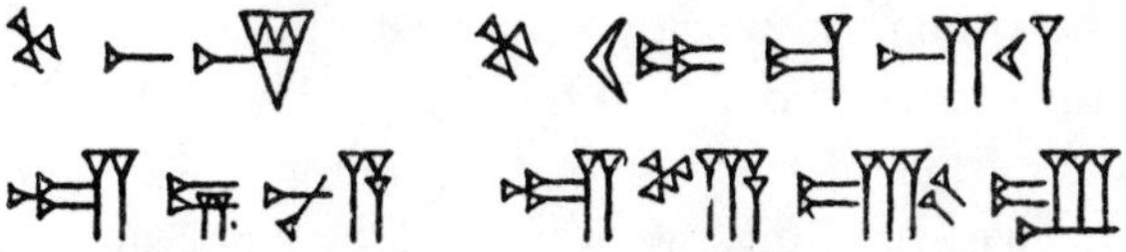

1. *māt Aš-šur* (ASSYRIA) 2. *māt Mi-iṣ-ri* (EGYPT)
3. ^{alu}*Ni-nu-a* (NINEVEH) 4. ^{alu}*Kar-ga-miš* (KARKHEMISH)

FIG. 25. The names of two countries and two cities, with determinatives

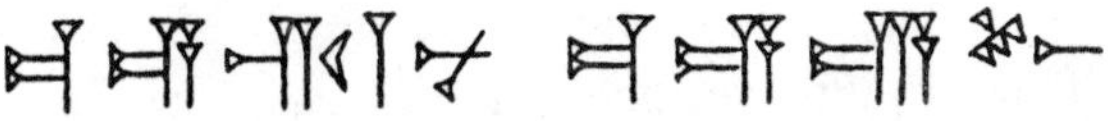

^{iṣu}*e-ri-nu* "CEDAR" ^{iṣu}*e-lip-pu* "SHIP"

FIG. 26. The name of a tree and of a wooden object, with determinative

^{erû}*pár-zil-lu* "IRON" ^{erû}*pa-a-šu* "AX"

FIG. 27. The name of a metal and of a metallic object, with determinative

before the names of cities, countries, trees and wooden objects, metals and metallic objects, etc. (Examples appear in Figs. 23–27.)

Like the ideograms, the determinatives also were identical in every language written with cuneiform characters. Thus, if we happen to find a text written in legible cuneiform script but in some unknown language, the names of men, women, gods, geographic names, etc. immediately reveal themselves as what they are because of their determinatives which are recognizable in that unknown language as well. Unlike our scripts, the cuneiform writing thus offers quite a number of clues to the reader, and also to the decipherer.

These facilities of reading or deciphering the cuneiform writing notwithstanding, we must not overlook an important difficulty of the reading of cuneiform writing, a difficulty that is produced by the *polyvalence* of many a sign. This polyvalence may consist in either of the following two situations:

(1) One and the same sign may be, under certain circumstances, an ideogram or a determinative or a phonetic syllable sign. Thus, the above mentioned  is in the first place a word-sign denoting the Sumerian word *an*, the Akkadian word *šamû*, both meaning "heaven," as well the Sumerian word *dingir* and the Akkadian word *ilu*, both meaning "god"; secondly, the same sign is a determinative used with names of deities, and thirdly, it is a phonetic symbol, representing the syllable *an*. Further examples are given in Fig. 28.

1. a) Word-sign (ideogram) for *iṣu* (wood)
   b) Determinative used before words denoting trees and wooden objects.
   c) Syllabic sign for *iz, is*, etc.
2. a) Word-sign (ideogram) for *mātu* (country) and *šadû* (mountain)
   b) Determinative used before names of countries and mountains.
   c) Syllabic sign for *kur, mat, šat, nat, gin*, etc.

FIG. 28. Written symbols which may be used as ideograms, determinatives and syllabic signs.

(2) The second type of polyvalence, which occurs less frequently in the earlier cuneiform script, but very often in the Neo-Assyrian and Neo-Babylonian writing, consists in what

is termed the *polyphony* of the cuneiform characters, viz., that *several phonetically different syllables* may be represented by one and the same sign, as illustrated by the few examples shown in Fig. 29. Thus, the sign meaning *bar* may be read also as *maš*, the sign meaning *ud* may stand also for *tam* or *par* or *laḫ* or *ḫiš*, the sign meaning *kid* may be read also as *saḫ* or *lil*, etc. The reader must rely on his knowledge of the language and on his familiarity with that particular kind of text in order to decide more or less accurately which syllabic value is the right one in the given grammatical or syntactical situation.

1. *kid, saḫ, lil.* 2. *piš, gir* 3. *lal, lib, lub, paḫ, nar*

FIG. 29. Characters representing several different syllables (polyphony).

The modern reader is likely to wonder also in connection with the cuneiform writing why the Babylonians did not discard their complicated system of partly polyvalent written characters and develop at least a simple and clear syllabic writing. The fact is that such attempts were made in the late Neo-Babylonian era, and it may well be assumed that the Semitic system of alphabetic writing, already known then in Babylonia, too, was taken in consideration as a pattern. But by that time it was too late—the cuneiform writing was just about to yield the stage to the more convenient alphabetic script. At any rate, in the heyday of the cuneiform writing, its users knew no alien script more convenient to handle and capable of exerting a stimulating influence in this direction, and all the inconveniences notwithstanding, the cuneiform script was still relatively the most convenient way of writing the Sumerian, Akkadian and other Near Eastern languages. The conclusion that it was a fairly convenient way, more convenient in any case than the Egyptian writing, is demonstrated by the very fact that the cuneiform script, unlike the Egyptian system of writing, did not remain confined to its native land but was adopted by a number of neighboring races for the writing of their quite different languages. People of the modern era have therefore not been very wrong in referring to the cuneiform writing occasionally as the "Roman letters of the ancient Orient." I shall now present a brief summary of these adoptions of the Babylonian cuneiform writing by other races, and then I shall say a few words about its historical and cultural significance.

(c) *The Spread of Cuneiform Writing to the East and to the West*

The influence exerted by the Babylonian civilization and script to the east of Babylonia was slight. In those parts, Elam, a state in southwestern Iran, was the only nation in contact with the Sumerian, later Babylonian, civilization; that contact started in the middle of the third millennium B.C., and in ancient times the Elamites borrowed not only the cuneiform script but also the Akkadian tongue for recording their documents. Only later did they decide to write texts in their own Elamite language, a tongue neither Indo-European nor Semitic, using the Babylonian cuneiform characters. In the first millennium B.C., when after the Medes the Indo-European Persians entered Iran from Armenia, Elam was their first cultural center. Thus, the Persians retained at first the Elamite written language along with the Elamite government, and only under Darius did they create an "Early Persian" script which was composed of wedge shapes but was a not quite pure alphabetic writing (cf. also pp. 50 et seq.). Their inscriptions in honor of their rulers were thereafter composed in *three languages: Old Persian, Akkadian* and *Elamite.*

The cultural influence of Babylon toward the west was stronger. The Babylonian cuneiform writing was first adopted to the west of Babylon, in the early part of the second millennium B.C., by the *Hurrians* of northwestern Mesopotamia. The Hurrians borrowed the cuneiform script for writing their language, a tongue neither Semitic nor Indo-European, and they soon passed it on to the nations of ancient Asia Minor which were culturally, in particular religiously, strongly dependent on them, and thus first of all to the *Hittites*, the dominant race of Asia Minor, of Indo-European origin and speakers of an Indo-European language. The Hittites, in turn, adopted the Babylonian cuneiform script to write not only their own language, but also the languages of their likewise Indo-European neighbors, the *Luwians* and *Palaians*, as well as the non-Indo-European tongue of the *Khattians* (or *Proto-Hattians*), the ancient race which founded a civilization of its own around the city of Khatti (or Ḫatti), the present-day Boğaz-köy, in the third millennium B.C., and later bequeathed it to the conquering Indo-European Hittites. Finally, the inhabitants of the land of *Urartu*, in the mountains of Armenia, were young collateral relatives of the Hurrians. From the 9th to 6th century B.C., the Urartaeans wrote their own language with the Neo-Assyrian cuneiform characters, in other words in a script imported from Assyria in all likelihood in that late period of their history only.

(d) *Remarks concerning the History and Civilization of the Hurrians and Hittites*

A few remarks concerning the history of the "Western races" seem to be indicated here. The *Hurrians* appear to have come forth from the Armenian mountains, to migrate toward northwestern Mesopotamia about 2000 B.C., and although they were not an Indo-European race themselves, they seem to have been led mostly by an Indo-European ruling class, of a specifically Indic character. Their conquests took them to Syria and Palestine, and probably also far into eastern Asia Minor. It is not clear yet whether there was any link between the Hurrians and the empire of the Hyksos in Egypt as well. The Hurrians founded small states all over, which disappeared quickly again; only the kingdom of Mitanni was temporarily more powerful under King Tušratta, about 1400 B.C. But Tušratta was defeated by King Šuppiluliuma of the Hittites about 1375 B.C., and Mitanni lost its importance, and soon its political independence, too. The ascending state of Assyria conquered the land and adopted the traditions of the Hurrians, including their desire to reach the Mediterranean.

The Hurrians played an important role in the history of the Near East, for in all probability they were the ones who imported the horse from southeastern Europe and popularized its breeding and use in that part of the Orient. In the domain of religion, a strong Hurrian influence on the *Hittites* is unmistakable. They must have been the ones who passed the Babylonian cuneiform writing, which they had taken over from Babylonia, on to the Hittites, and the latter obtained from the Hurrians also various intellectual assets, Hurrian and Babylonian myths and epics, such as the Gilgamesh Epic, along with the script.

The Hurrians vanished from the stage of history by 1000 B.C., at the latest, and only in the land of Urartu, in the mountains of Armenia, did the racially cognate race of the Urartaeans maintain its position as a rival on equal footing of the Neo-Assyrian empire from the 10th to the 7th century B.C., to be eventually supplanted by the Indo-European Armenians in the 6th century B.C. The Urartaeans, who excelled in the art of the working of metals, conducted military campaigns which took them deep into the Caucasus, too, so that inscriptions in the Urartaean tongue, written in the Neo-Assyrian cuneiform script, are being discovered not only in eastern Anatolia and northwestern Iran, but also in what is Soviet territory today.

In eastern Asia Minor (Cappadocia), the civilization of the *Khattians* (or *Proto-Hattians*), a non-Indo-European race, developed around the city of Khatti, or Ḫatti or Hattuša, about 2000 B.C., or even earlier. It was taken over by the conquering *Hittites*, an Indo-European race, in the early part of the second millennium B.C. The Hittites had migrated to Cappadocia from Europe, by some still unknown way, and they fused with the Proto-Hattians. The Hittite language, an Indo-European tongue, became the dominant vernacular, but Proto-Hattian retained its importance as the language of the cults of the most important state deities. The Hittites were the dominant power of the Near East notably in the 14th and 13th centuries B.C. Their king Šuppiluliuma (about 1380–1350 B.C.) destroyed the Hurrian kingdom of Mitanni and commanded the respect of Egypt as well. His son, Muršili II (about 1345–1315 B.C.), fought bitter wars against Arzawa and other kingdoms in Asia Minor to defend the hegemony won by his father. Hattušili III (about 1282–1250 B.C.) ended a long war with Egypt by signing the peace treaty with Ramses II of Egypt which we mentioned before (p. 4). The Hittite empire in Asia Minor crumbled under the onslaught of the barbarian "Sea Peoples" (cf. p. 4) about 1200 B.C. Only in northern Syria did the so-called "*Neo-Hittites*" survive until the 8th century B.C., as witnessed by their inscriptions in the so-called "Hittite hieroglyphic" script (cf. pp. 69 *et seq.*), notably in the city of Karkhemish at the bend of the Euphrates in Syria, but they were eventually absorbed in the expanding Assyrian empire.

(e) *Alphabetic Scripts Based on the Cuneiform Writing*

Aside from the outright borrowings of the Babylonian cuneiform writing by races speaking other tongues, we know of two more cases of the creation in the ancient Orient of new scripts utilizing the wedge shape as their basic element. In the city of *Ugarit* on the northern Syrian coast, today the heap of ruins called Ras Shamrah, French excavations, begun in 1929, have unearthed the center of a small state inhabited by a Western Semitic populace. However, Ugarit, as a harbor town, was subject also to alien, Hurrian and even Cretan, influences. As for the history of Ugarit, not much more is known today than the fact that its king became a vassal of the Hittite monarch Šuppiluliuma, probably after the defeat of Tušratta. In the domain of literature, of great significance is the discovery of a number of clay tablets in the library of a temple, bearing Ugaritic mythological texts, epic poems in the Ugaritic language, honoring their deities; these tablets date from approximately the 15th or 14th century B.C. These texts appear on clay tablets, and also the shape of the script resembles the cuneiform writing. But the Ugaritic script is an *alphabetic system,* using only thirty signs (without any word-signs or determinatives), and is the oldest specimen of alphabetic writing in the Near East (cf. Fig. 30). The findings of the most recent years point to the conclusion that the Semitic alphabet of individual letter signs was already known to the people of Ugarit, in the same sequence in which it is known to us from later times and which influenced the conventional arrangement of the European alphabets.

The youngest script based on the wedge shape was invented by the *Persians* under the great Darius. The Early Persian writing, as used in the Old Persion portions of the trilingual inscriptions in honor of the ancient Persian rulers, has only one feature in common with the Babylonian cunei-

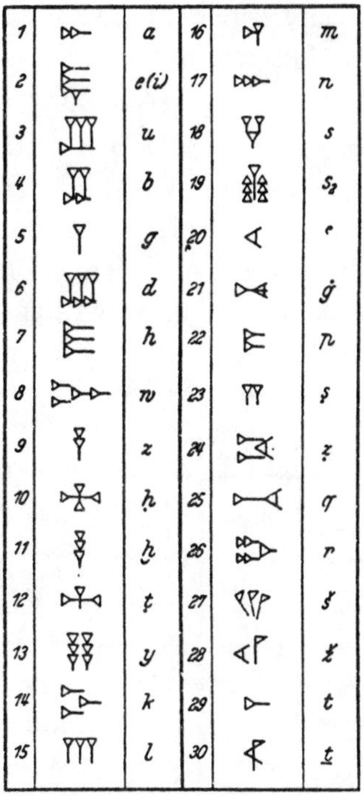
1 a
2 e(i)
3 u
4 b
5 g
6 d
7 h
8 w
9 z
10 ḥ
11 ḫ
12 ṭ
13 y
14 k
15 l
16 m
17 n
18 s
19 s_2
20 ʿ
21 ġ
22 p
23 ṣ
24 ẓ
25 q
26 r
27 š
28 ṯ
29 t
30 ṯ

FIG. 30. The Ugaritic alphabet. (De Langhe, *Les Textes de Ras Shamra-Ugarit*, vol. I, p. 243.)

form script, viz., the wedge shape which constitutes the principal element of the characters. But this is a mere external resemblance, because the Early Persian script is an alphabetic system, although not quite purely alphabetic. It consists of thirty-six phonetic symbols, and it still shows a few elements of the syllabic system of writing (cf. Fig. 31). A few additionally created ideograms are obviously artificial. The Semitic alphabetic writing, known to the Persians in its Aramaic variant, was indubitably a factor of great influence on the creation of this script.

(f) *The Decipherment of the Early Persian Cuneiform Script*

We have followed the development of the cuneiform writing from its origin as a Sumerian pictographic script, throughout its dissemination over the Near East, until its second heyday in ancient Persia. In order to describe the progress of the decipherment of the cuneiform script and of the reconstruction of the languages written by it, we must

Symbol	Phonetic Value	Symbol	Phonetic Value	Symbol	Phonetic Value	Symbol	Phonetic Value
𐎠	*a, ā*	𐎩	*ǧ, ǧa*	𐎲	*b, ba*	𐎻	*w before i, wī*
𐎡	*i, ī*	𐎪	*ǧ before i, ǧī*	𐎳	*f, fa*	𐎼	*r, ra*
𐎢	*u, ū*	𐎫	*t, ta*	𐎴	*n, na*	𐎽	*r before u, rū*
𐎣	*k, ka*	𐎬	*t before u, tū*	𐎵	*n before u, nū*	𐎾	*l, la*
𐎤	*k before u, kū*	𐎭	*d, da*	𐎶	*m, ma*	𐎿	*s, sa*
𐎥	*g, ga*	𐎮	*d before i, dī*	𐎷	*m before i, mī*	𐏀	*z, za*
𐎦	*g before u, gū*	𐎯	*d before u, dū*	𐎸	*m before u, mū*	𐏁	*š, ša*
𐎧	*ḫ, ḫa*	𐎰	*ϑ, ϑa*	𐎹	*y, ya*	𐏂	*ϑr, ϑra*
𐎨	*č, ča*	𐎱	*p, pa*	𐎺	*w, wa*	𐏃	*h, ha*

FIG. 31. The Early Persian alphabet. (Jensen, *Die Schrift*, Fig. 69.)

follow the opposite course and contemplate, first of all, the Early Persian script which, being an alphabetic system, is more readily susceptible to decipherment, and only then are we to proceed to unravel the enigma of the other languages in the chronological order of their decipherment.

I must point out, however, before proceeding any further that the knowledge of the cuneiform writing was lost much earlier than that of the Egyptian hieroglyphics. Even the Greeks had no longer any correct notion of it; only Herodotus (IV, 87) mentions it as 'Ασσύρια γράμματα (Assýria grámmata), "Assyrian characters." Thus only in the modern era, beginning roughly in the early 17th century A.D., did Europe begin to hear about this "nail-shaped" (as it was first called) script, through the reports of individual travellers. The first report with a short specimen of the script, consisting of five groups of symbols, was contained in a letter written by Pietro della Valle from the city of Shiras in Persia to a friend in Naples in 1621. The first reproduction of a complete Early Persian inscription was made public by Chardin in 1674. The name "*Keilschrift*" (cuneiform writing) seems to have been used first by Engelbert Kämpfer in the late 17th century.

In the course of the 18th century, other explorers reported on several inscriptions honoring kings of ancient Persia, in their complete trilingual form, and in 1762, Count Caylus even published a report on a quadrilingual (Old Persian, Elamite, Babylonian and Egyptian) alabaster vase of Xerxes, but since even the Egyptian writing was still undeciphered in those days, a decipherment of the cuneiform characters was out of the question. Carsten Niebuhr brought back especially reliable copies of trilingual inscriptions from his trip to Persepolis in 1765, and he published them in 1788. Niebuhr already recognized the three completely different systems of writing in the inscriptions, viz., first, a quite simple script (Early Persian) consisting of altogether forty-two characters (according to Niebuhr's count), secondly, a somewhat more complicated writing (the Elamite script), and thirdly, one especially rich in characters (the Babylonian cuneiform writing).

Following in Niebuhr's footsteps, Olav Gerhard Tychsen, the Orientalist from Rostock, made an important discovery in 1798: He established the fact that in the first, simplest, script a single diagonal wedge served as a sign separating two words from each other. Another important accomplishment of Tychsen (among several mistaken conclusions) was the assumption that the three scripts represented three different languages.

Another step forward was accomplished by the Danish academician Friedrich Münter, by his *Versuch über die keilförmigen Inschriften zu Persepolis,** in 1802. Working independently from Tychsen, he also interpreted the single diagonal wedge as a separation mark between words, and he presented plausible historical arguments to warrant the conclusion that the inscriptions in question originated under the Old Persian monarchs of the House of the Achaemenides, and that therefore their language should be close to that of the Avesta, the sacred book of Persia. He suspected, furthermore, that the first portions of the inscriptions were in an alphabetic script, the second portions in a syllabic script, and the third portions consisted of ideographic word-signs. He reasoned that all the three portions of any given inscription were probably identical in content, for multilingual inscriptions had been a very common custom in the ancient world, and also because whenever a word recurred in the first portion of an inscription, a corresponding recurrence of symbols could be observed every time in the second and third portions of the same inscription as well. He assumed, quite

* An Essay on the Cuneiform Inscriptions of Persepolis.

correctly, that certain repeatedly recurring groups of symbols meant "King" and "King of Kings." He was less lucky in his attempt at determining the phonetic values of the characters; only by sheer accident did he identify the symbols for a and *b* correctly.

The man who succeeded in making the Early Persian script really legible, beyond such rudimentary findings, however, was no trained Orientalist, but a young German high-school teacher, Georg Friedrich Grotefend (1775–1853) of Göttingen. He was practically ignorant of Oriental languages, but he had practiced diligently the decipherment of artificially composed secret scripts. His situation was thus totally different from that of Champollion: Champollion spent fifteen years in painstaking studying and preliminary training, after which he succeeded almost despite expectations, whereas Grotefend plunged right into the project, without any great preliminary training, and without a bilingual inscription to go by, such as there were available for the study of Egyptian, and yet it took him a mere few weeks to score quite a considerable success. At any rate, however, Grotefend also had to have certain auxiliary data available, for no decipherment is feasible without some clues to go by. Also Grotefend recognized the separation mark and the three types of writing. And also he deduced that the first portion of each inscription was written in an alphabetic, not a syllabic, script because there often were as many as ten symbols between two successive separation marks, and the existence of words of ten syllables was an improbability.

His actual decipherment, presented before the Learned Society of Göttingen on September 4, 1802, was based on the inscriptions reproduced in our Figures 32 and 33. Like Münter, Grotefend assumed that the inscriptions had been composed by Persian kings of the family of the Achaemenides, and he conjectured also that the first portions of the inscription were written in Old Persian, the language of the reigning dynasty. Also Grotefend studied the inscriptions with the purpose of finding the names of the kings with their titles and genealogies, already known from other ancient sources, and specifically from sources in Iran itself, viz., from the inscriptions of the later Sassanian kings. And like Münter, also Grotefend tried to identify the word recurring in Fig. 32 under Nos. 2, 4, 5 and 6, and in Fig. 33 under Nos. 2, 4, 5 and 7, as the words meaning "king." He interpreted the second inscription, along the Sassanian pattern, tentatively as follows: "X, the King, the great (?), the King of Kings, Y's, the King's, son, the Achaemenide (?)—." The translation "Y's, the king's, son" was based on the considera-

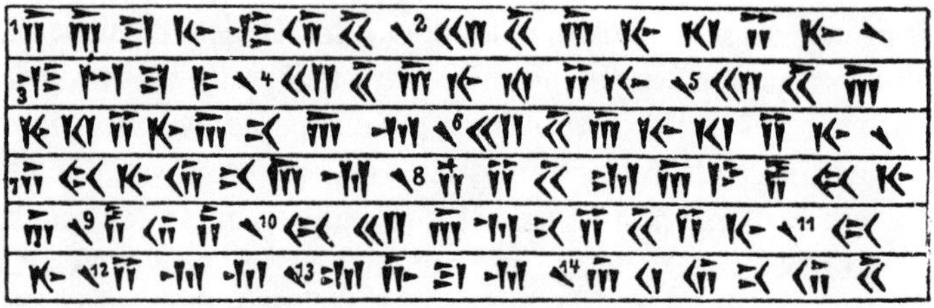

(Transliteration) (1) *D(a)-a-r(a)-y(a)-v(a)-u-š(a)* (2) *x(a)-š(a)-a-y(a)-ϑ(a)-i-y(a)* (3) *v(a)-z(a)-r(a)-k(a)* (4) *x(a)-š(a)-a-y(a)-ϑ(a)-i-y(a)* (5) *x(a)-š(a)-a-y(a)-ϑ(a)-i-y(a)-a-n(a)-a-m(a)* (6) *x(a)-š(a)-a-y(a)-ϑ(a)-i-y(a)* (7) *d(a)-h(a)-y(a)-u-n(a)-a-m(a)* (8) *Vi-i-š(a)-t(a)-a-s(a)-p(a)-h(a)-y(a)-a* (9) *p(a)-u-ç(a)* (10) *H(a)-x(a)-a-m(a)-n(a)-i-š(a)-i-y(a)* (11) *h(a)-y(a)* (12) *i-m(a)-m(a)* (13) *t(a)-č(a)-r(a)-m(a)* (14) *a-ku-u-n(a)-u-š(a)*

(Pronunciation) *Dārayavauš xšāyaϑiya vazrka xšāyaϑiya xšāyaϑiyānām xšāyaϑiya dahyunām Vištāspahya puça Haxāmanišiya hya imam tačaram akunauš**

* x = ch in German ach; š = sh in English *she*; y as in English *yes*; *θ* = *th* in English *the*; č = ch in English *chin*; ç as in French ça.

"Darius, the great king, the king of kings, the king of the lands, Hystaspes' son, the Achaemenide, (is the one) who built this palace."

FIG. 32. Old Persian inscription of Darius. (Messerschmidt, *Die Entzifferung der Keilschrift*, Fig. 1.)

tion that the word "Y" of the second inscription appeared at the beginning of the first inscription, thus in all probability as the name of a ruler, but it appeared in the second inscription after the title "King of Kings" with an ending augmented by one sign; Grotefend concluded from this circumstance that he was looking at a possessive case linked as such with the subsequent word meaning "son."

As the next step, Grotefend went through the list of the names of the Persian kings, known from Herodotus, and checked which names seemed to be most likely to be represented by the characters appearing in the inscriptions. Cyrus and Cambyses seemed to be out of the question because the two names under study did not begin with the same letter, and also because they were not of different lengths, but approximately equal in length. Finally, an important fact was that the father of the author of the second inscription, who was the author of the first inscription, also bore the title "king," *whereas the father of the first inscription did not.* All

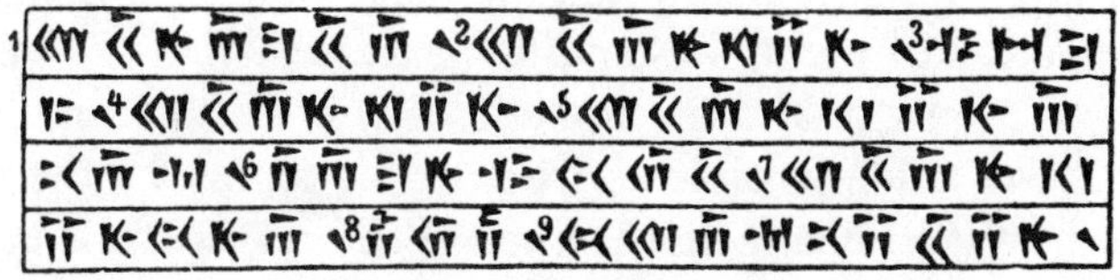

(Transliteration) *X(a)-š(a)-y(a)-a-r(a)-š(a)-a* (2) *x(a)-š(a)-a-y(a)-ϑ(a)-i-y(a)* (3) *v(a)-z(a)-r(a)-k(a)* (4) *x(a)-š(a)-a-y(a)-ϑ(a)-i-y(a)* (5) *x(a)-š(a)-a-y(a)-ϑ(a)-i-y(a)-a-n(a)-a-m(a)* (6) *D(a)-a-r(a)-y(a)-v(a)-h(a)-u-š(a)* (7) *x(a)-š(a)-a-y(a)-ϑ(a)-i-y(a)-h(a)-y(a)-a* (8) *p(a)-u-ç(a)* (9) *H(a)-x(a)-a-m(a)-n(a)-i-š(a)-i-y(a)*

(Pronunciation) *Xšayāršā xšāyaϑiya vazrka xšāyaϑiya xšāyaϑiyānām Dārayavahauš xšāyaϑiyahya puça Haxāmanišiya*

"Xerxes, the great king, the king of kings, Darius', the king's, son, the Achaemenide."

FIG. 33. Old Persian inscription of Xerxes. (Messerschmidt, *Die Entzifferung der Keilschrift*, Fig. 2.)

these facts considered together led to the conclusion that *the author of the second inscription must have been Xerxes* and *the author of the first inscription must have been his father, Darius*, whose father, Hystaspes, *had not been a king*. The next logical step was to find the Persian forms of these three names, which were presumably somewhat different from the forms handed down by the Greeks. Grotefend inserted the Avestic forms of the names, and thus he succeeded in determining the phonetic values of 15 letters—although four of those 15 were incorrect because he failed to establish the exact forms of the Old Persian variants of the names. With the phonetic values thus obtained, he attempted to read the word meaning "king," arriving at the pronunciation *khsheh* . . . (instead of the correct sound, xšāyaθiya). The reading and translation of the two inscriptions deciphered by Grotefend is also shown in Figs. 32 and 33.

Grotefend thus succeeded within a very short time, without any bilingual inscription to help him, in laying the foundation of the understanding of texts written in characters of totally unknown phonetic values. This accomplishment was made possible, apart from his genius, by the fact that he was familiar with the line of Persian kings from other sources, as well as by the fact that the Early Persian script consisted of only thirty-nine characters and was constructed along principles akin to those underlying our alphabetic scripts. In the case of a syllabic writing, using a greater number of symbols, the range of possible phonetic values would have been much wider, and the prospect of finding the right values would have been poorer.

The fact that Grotefend's later activities no longer produced as happy results as his first decipherments is to be attributed not solely to his insufficient training as an Orientalist, but above all to the circumstance, emphasized by

Grotefend himself, that a *decipherer and an interpreter* (i.e., a philologist) *must not be mistaken for each other*. His decipherment should have been developed and elaborated further by trained, professional Orientalists, but those were the very people who failed to give him the credit that was his due. In fact, the scientific journal of Göttingen did not even print the full report of his discovery, but merely a short item mentioning it. Only in 1815 was there published a detailed report in Heeren's *Ideen über die Politik, den Verkehr und den Handel der vornehmsten Völker der alten Welt.** This is how it came about that his decipherment was given little attention and interest at first.

It was only in 1826 that the Danish professor Rask was able to identify the ending of the genitive plural in the phrase "king of kings," and only in 1836 could the phonetic values of most of the Early Persian characters in one of the inscriptions be defined by Burnouf, a French student of the Avesta, and still more completely by the German Christian Lassen, professor of Sanskrit in Bonn, on the ground of a list of peoples. Of particular importance was the further finding of Lassen that in the Early Persian script, similarly to the usage of the Indic alphabets, the vowel a was not indicated by any special sign (but ā was indicated by the addition of a), so that, e.g., a *p* may be read as the consonant *p* or as a sort of syllabic sign for *pa*. Thus, the ancient Persians wrote *xšayθiy vzrk* for *xšāyaθiya vazrka* ("the great king"), *hxamnišiy* for *Haxāmanišiya* ("the Achaemenid"), *daryvuš* for *Dārayavauš* ("Darius"), etc.

In the meantime, however, an English investigator went to work on the decipherment of the Early Persian writing, independently from Grotefend, and favorable circumstances enabled him to make substantially greater progress. Henry

* "Thoughts on the Politics, Communications and Commerce of the Most Outstanding Nations of the Ancient World."

Rawlinson (1810–1895), a British officer, entered the Persian government service as a military adviser in 1835, and as such he had the opportunity to undertake extensive journeys in the country and to study Early Persian inscriptions right in the field. Of decisive importance was his discovery of the big Darius inscription on the cliff of Bīsutūn (referred to mostly, incorrectly, as Behistun), by far the longest and most substantial of all Early Persian inscriptions. In 1835, he had only the sketchiest idea of Grotefend's decipherment; he had not even the opportunity to have the relevant publications sent to Persia. Thus, as he stated, he undertook the entire decipherment anew, independently on his own, along similar considerations. He used two other inscriptions, copied by him in his own hand; those two inscriptions were likewise records left by Darius and Xerxes, so that he reached the same conclusion as Grotefend. His knowledge of the Behistun inscription, however, permitted him to gain a better and more profound insight into the Old Persian language than Grotefend's. He soon recognized it as a close relative of the Avestic and Old Indic (Sanskrit) languages, and therefore he was able to use these languages for the interpretation of the Old Persian words and grammatical forms. In this case, it was possible also to achieve correct, incontestable results with the aid of simple homophones in the closely related languages, by what is called the *etymological method*, which is all too often misleading when the relationship between the languages under consideration is less close, as will be discussed later. The publication of the big Behistun inscription by Rawlinson in 1846 signified a milestone along the path of these researches and studies. Subsequently, the last details of the Early Persian script and the Old Persian language as well were cleared up during the following decades, by Rawlinson, Hincks (the Irishman whom I already mentioned in connection with the Egyptian writing, and whom I shall mention again in discussing the decipherment of the Babylonian-Assyrian script) and Jules Oppert, of Paris.

(g) *The Decipherment of the Neo-Elamite Cuneiform Script*

After the unlocking of the secret of Old Persian, the language written in an alphabetic script and closely related to Avestic and Old Indic, the trilingual inscriptions of the Achaemenids could be regarded as records written in three languages one of which was known, so that the decipherment of the other two languages appeared to be easy on the basis of its knowledge. The second portion of each inscription, evidently written in a syllabic script (the *Neo-Elamite* version, as we know today), was logically the next to be deciphered, because even though this script with its 111 different characters seemed to be more complicated than the alphabetic Early Persian writing, it was still simpler than the writing used in the third portion, with its many hundreds of symbols. The *absence of separation marks* between words turned out to be an obstacle in the attempts at decipherment. Also when trying to decipher the Neo-Elamite portions of the Achaemenide inscriptions, the first step was to identify the corresponding names in the Early Persian and Neo-Elamite portions, followed by the interpolation of syllabic phonetic values in the Neo-Elamite text. The first attempt in this direction was made by Grotefend in 1837, and he established the fact that names of male persons were identified by a vertical wedge (the determinative for the names of male persons, as we put it today) placed before them. A better progress in this field was feasible only after the publication in 1853 of the Elamite text of the big Behistun inscription by Professor Norris of London, for it resulted in the increase of the number of proper names from the formerly known 40 to 90. The result was that the phonetic values of most of the Elamite syllable signs could be determined, and on the basis of the Old Persian translation also the individual words could be clarified lexically as well as grammatically. Nevertheless, during the subsequent decades the study of Elamite lagged far behind the study of the other languages written in cuneiform characters, and there are still several unclarified points in the Elamite grammar.

(h) *The Decipherment of the Babylonian Cuneiform Script*

The investigators turned with far greater interest to the study of the third and most complicated portions of the Achaemenid inscriptions, the *Babylonian-Assyrian* (*Akkadian*) parts. It so happened that it had been established in the meantime that the same script had been used on monuments as well as on clay tablets, many of which became known by the end of the 18th century A.D., to be followed by an unending series of discoveries of more and more such relics in the 19th century. Thus there seemed to exist a whole rich literature in that language, in sharp contrast to the conditions relative to the Early Persian and Neo-Elamite versions. But the world could finally look forward to the revelation of the most important historical and cultural data about ancient Babylonia and Assyria when the French Consul Botta began, in 1843, the excavation of the palace of the Assyrian king Sargon in Khorsabad, and again in 1845 when the Englishman Layard began to excavate the ruins of Nineveh, for both excavations unearthed a great many monuments inscribed in the same third variant of cuneiform writing.

The Achaemenid inscriptions had to be used as the point of departure also in the endeavor to decipher this most important language of the entire literature written in cuneiform characters, and the first step had to be once again the attempt to identify the Akkadian equivalents of the *proper names* occurring in the Old Persian version and then to use them for the determination of the phonetic values of syllable signs. Of course, that was easier said than done. Not only did the writing contain more than 300 different signs, and not only was there no separation mark at all, but—as today we know—one and the same word was written in one instance by several phonetic syllable signs and in another instance by an ideographic word-sign, and the system of ideographic representation extended even to the writing of proper names. Such a peculiar system of writing was obviously bound to discourage the first investigators who had absolutely no knowledge of this writing convention. Thus, Rawlinson himself made the following admission, in 1850, when he had already been able to interpret a longer historical inscription correctly as to its essential points: "I will admit freely that when I had learned the secret of every single Babylonian symbol and every single Babylonian word to which I had found any clue at all in the trilingual inscriptions, whether by direct evidence or through a key, when I tried then to apply the key thus gained to the interpretation of the Assyrian inscriptions, I was tempted more than once to give up these studies once and for all, because I was losing all hope for the achievement of any satisfactory result."

For the better understanding of the reader, I reproduce here the original text of an inscription, with its transliteration and translation (Fig. 34); this text is the Babylonian portion of the Xerxes inscription, the Old Persian text of which is shown in Fig. 33 on page 55. As in the Old Persian text, the equivalent of the word "king" can be recognized to be represented by the *ideographic word-sign* recurring under the numbers 2, 4, 5 and 8. Thus, according to the pattern of the Old Persian version, the two symbols appearing under No. 3 must mean "great" (read today as rabû^{ú}, i.e., *rabû*, "great" with the *phonetic complement* "ú"), whereas the first six symbols in the first line must stand for the name of Xerxes (read today as ^{I}*Ḫi-ši-ʾ-ar-ši*). The vertical wedge at the beginning of the first line revealed itself as the determinative used before the names of male persons, which Grotefend had already recognized as such. The same determinative appears

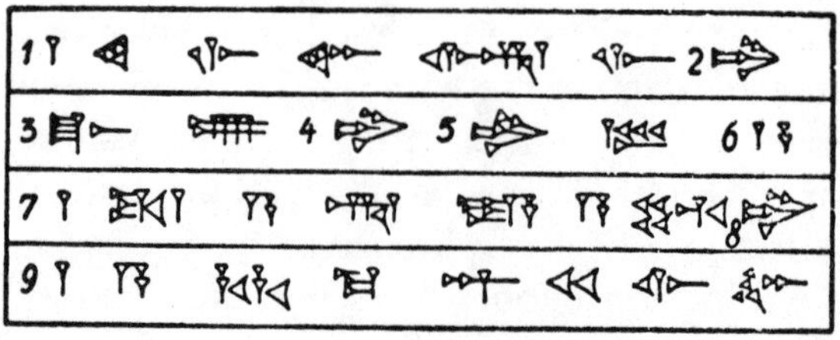

(1) ^{I}*Ḫi-ši-ʾ-ar-ši* (2) *šarru* (3) *rabûᵘ* (4) *šar* (5) *šarrāni*^{MEŠ} (6) *mār* (7) ^{I}*Da-a-ri-ia-a-muš* (8) *šarri* (9) *A-ḫa-ma-an-niš-ši-ʾ*

"Xerxes, the great king, the king of kings, the son of Darius the king, the Achaemenide."

FIG. 34. Babylonian inscription of Xerxes. (Meissner, *Die Keilschrift*, Fig. 3.)

before No. 7 = "Darius" (^{I}*Da-a-ri-ia-a-muš*) and before No. 9 = "Achaemenide" (^{I}*A-ḫa-ma-an-niš-ši-ʾ*). The word meaning "son" cannot follow the name of Darius in this version, as it did in the Old Persian text, but must precede it (as No. 6) whereas the symbol *preceding* No. 6 indicates the *plural* of the word "king" (plural sign, MEŠ).

The meaning of each individual word was thus ascertained, but still regardless of its pronunciation. For the determination of the spoken sounds, it was again necessary to use the proper names as the point of departure, for the proper names could not be represented by ideographic word-signs, but had to be in syllable signs, since the name of Xerxes consisted of five characters, and the name of Darius consisted of six, not counting the determinative. The determination of the phonetic values of these syllable signs seemed nevertheless difficult, for the Babylonian forms of these names might have sounded different from the Persian versions. (In fact, as we know now, they did actually sound different.) Another difficulty consisted in the fact that many of the signs appearing on the clay tablets from Babylon were different, often sharply different, in shape from the forms used in the Achaemenid inscriptions; we have already pointed out the sharp differences among the Old, Middle and New, Babylonian and Assyrian cuneiform scripts (cf. pages 35 *et seq.*). Thus, the investigators of the cuneiform writing faced here a problem similar to the one which confronted Champollion as he compared the hieroglyphic, hieratic and demotic characters.

It is impossible to mention here more than the most important points of the widely ramified detail work, of no significance for the general public, involved in the decipherment. In the 1840's, Grotefend identified the names of Darius, Xerxes, Cyrus and Hystaspes in the Babylonian texts, and he realized also that a group of symbols appearing on bricks found in Babylonia had to represent the name of Nebuchadnezzar—only he was unable to read it as yet. (Cf. pp. 53 *et seq.*).

The Swedish Isidor Löwenstern was the first to advocate the view (in 1845) that this was a Semitic language. He was of the opinion that the phonetic symbols of the Babylonian cuneiform writing were simple consonant signs, because—he argued—also the later Semitic alphabetic writings (the Hebrew writing, the Arabic writing, etc.) indicated the consonants only, leaving the vowels unrecorded. In advocating this view, however, he made the peculiar observation that for every consonant there had existed several, apparently indiscriminately interchangeable signs. Thus, for instance, he found no less than seven different signs representing *r*—which actually are the syllable signs *ar*, *ir*, *er*, *ur*, *ra*, *ri* and *ru*.

The brilliant Edward Hincks, whose name I have mentioned repeatedly on the preceding pages, was the man who recognized that these signs did not represent consonants, but syllables. In 1850, he was able to state decisively that the Babylonian cuneiform writing contained "not one single sign standing for a simple consonant, but signs representing a consonant preceded or followed by a vowel." Hincks ascertained also that in addition to the "simple" syllable signs of the *ab*, *ir*, etc. and *da*, *ki*, etc. type, the script contained also symbols for the complex consonant + vowel + consonant type, such as *kan*, *mur*, etc., and that each such complex sign could be split into two simple ones (i.e., *ka-an*, *mu-ur*, etc.), for these two methods of writing alternated in frequently recurring words (cf. Fig. 35). Hincks is the discoverer also of the polyvalence of the Babylonian cuneiform symbols; he saw that the same sign could be used as a word-sign, a syllable sign or determinative, and he recognized also the determinatives of names of deities, countries and cities, etc. correctly as such.

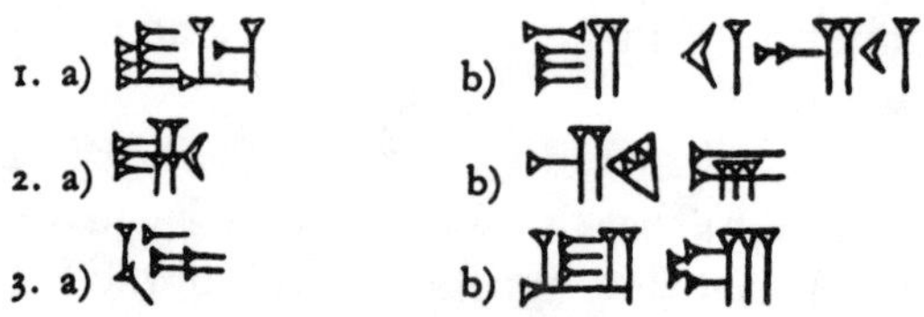

1. a) *šar* = b) *ša-ar*
2. a) *gir* = b) *gi-ir*
3. a) *lum* = b) *lu-um*

FIG. 35. Alternative compound and simple syllable symbols.

Botta, the excavator of the palace of Sargon in Khorsabad, is the man to whom the principal credit is due for the recognition that one and the same word could be represented in one instance by one single ideograph word-sign and in another instance by a group of symbols which must be regarded as syllable signs. This conclusion was warranted by the fact that among the numerous inscriptions in the palace of Sargon there were quite a few which were identical in content, and it was a frequent experience to find a group of phonetic symbols in one of them at a place where an ideogram appeared in another. Thus also the spoken words represented by ideograms could gradually be determined.

A final important point of knowledge was discovered by Rawlinson who was in the position to work with abundant material, and who is fully deserving of the honorary title, "Father of Assyriology," given to him by the British. The important point to which I refer here is the peculiarity known as *phonetical polyphony*, the fact that the symbol 𒌓, meaning *ud*, can be read also as *tam*, *par*, *laḫ*, or *ḫiš* (cf. page 43). He was in the position to state in his publication on the Babylonian text of the Behistun inscription (1851) that, "It can be proven beyond all doubt that the very great majority of the Assyrian symbols are polyphonous." The list of 246 characters which he included in that publication is on the whole still valid today and is the basis of our current lists of characters.

The reading of the proper names still remained the hardest nut to crack for a long time to come. Thus, the name of Nebuchadnezzar, *Nabû-kudurrī-uṣur* ("O /God/ Nabû, protect my boundary mark"), appeared written as AN.AK.ŠA.DU.ŠIŠ; *Šulmānu-ašarid*, Salmanassar, was written as DI.MA.NU.BAR. The difficulty was solved only when vocabularies of the ancient Babylonian savants were discovered in Nineveh, in which such ideographic methods of writing were explained. It was seen then that AN.AK was an ideographic symbol for the name of the god ^{d}*Na-bi-um*, SA.DU represented the word *kudurru* (boundary mark), SIS stood for *naṣāru* (to protect), the imperative form of which was *uṣur*, DI was the ideographic symbol for *šulmu* (welfare)—thus DI-*ma-nu* stood for *šulmānu* = gift of welcome—and BAR represented *ašaridu* (first). Generally speaking, without the grammatical, lexical and graphic lists prepared by the ancient Babylonians and Assyrians themselves on their language, the decipherment of the Babylonian cuneiform writing would probably have been a more laborious task than it actually was.

At any rate, an adequate basis for the reading and translation of the Akkadian language was created about the middle of the 19th century A.D., and the framework erected merely had to be completed by details. Hincks had recognized even formerly that two inscriptions, one written in Old Babylonian script, the other in Neo-Babylonian characters, were duplicates of each other. This discovery enabled him to compare a whole series of Old Babylonian signs with their Neo-Babylonian equivalents and thus to lay the groundwork for a cuneiform palaeography.

The subsequent research made very rapid headway, and it is truly amazing how little time was needed to achieve a complete understanding of the texts. Of course, investigators less close to the subject still maintained an attitude of scepticism about polyphony and ideography, not known to them from the more familiar systems of writing, and consequently they still distrusted the new science. In order to settle the question of the reliability of the decipherment, the Royal Asiatic Society of London therefore resorted to a special expedient: In 1857, Rawlinson, Hincks, Fox Talbot and Oppert happened to be in London at the same time. All the four scholars were given a copy of a longer text which had just been discovered, with the request that they work on it independently from each other. Their letters were then opened in a formal meeting, and the Society was able to find with satisfaction that all the four solutions agreed in all their essential points. Thus the young science of Assyriology could now truly be said to stand on a firm foundation.

Decipherment was no longer a much discussed subject in the further course of the research. In the second half of the 19th century and in the early years of the 20th, careful detail work was the main thing and it eventually built Assyriology up to a full-fledged philological science. The Semitic character of the language having been firmly established, wide use was made also of the phonetically identical or similar words of the Hebrew and Arabic languages for the determination of the meanings of Akkadian words. And in fact, there were many words found which were totally identical in sound and in meaning in Akkadian, Hebrew and Arabic, such as, e.g., the Hebrew and Akkadian *kī* (how); the Akkadian and Arabic *lā* and the Hebrew *lō* (not); the Akkadian *bītu*, the Arabic *baitu* and the Hebrew *bajit* or *bēt* (house); the Akkadian and Arabic *kalbu* and the Hebrew *keleb* (dog); the Akkadian *šarāpu* and the Hebrew *šāraf* (to burn); the Akkadian *ebēru* and the Hebrew *'ābar* (to transgress); etc. Only occasionally will the meanings differ, as e.g., in the case of the Akkadian *amāru* (to see) and the Hebrew *'āmar* (to say). Thus, the *etymological method*, the determination of the meanings of words of an unknown language according to the meanings of phonetically identical or similar words of a known related language, was in most instances successful in the domain of the Akkadian tongue.

The German scholar Friedrich Delitzsch, who founded a strongly methodistic school in Leipzig, Breslau and Berlin and made Germany the center of cuneiform research, was the chief Assyrian philologist about 1900. That was when also the Americans began to be interested in the new science, and the first representatives of the now highly developed American Assyriology were trained then by Delitzsch in Germany.

The 20th century learned, above all, to divide the disuniform structure of the Akkadian language spatially and temporally into distinct Babylonian and Assyrian dialect groups. The fruit of this research, encouraged chiefly by Benno Landsberger, is the *Grundriss der akkadischen Grammatik*,* a book evidencing amazing diligence and knowledge, by Wolfram von Soden, published by the Papal Bible Institute in Rome in 1952. A dictionary of modest size, also by Wolfram von Soden, can be expected to be published within a few years. Thus, German science has an honorable share in having produced the present broad structure of Assyriology.

(i) *The Interpretation of Sumerian Records*

Akkadian was the last of the languages of cuneiform literature the decipherment of which had to begin with the most fundamental details. The translation of Sumerian does not mean the decipherment of a new script, but merely the interpretation of another language, for Sumerian was written in the same Babylonian cuneiform script as Akkadian. This translation of the Sumerian language was accomplished very slowly and gradually. In fact, in the first decades of the history of Assyriology it was even doubted that Sumerian had been a distinct language at all, rather than just a mystic way of writing Akkadian. As late as in the last decade of the 19th century, young F. H. Weissbach found it necessary to devote a book, *Die sumerische Frage*** (Leipzig, 1898), to proving that Sumerian had been a distinct language.

But there were many difficulties even about the purely linguistic understanding of Sumerian. This peculiar language, heretofore not considered definitely related with any known tongue, became extinct as a living vernacular soon after Hammurabi's time and continued to be used only by

* An Outline of Akkadian Grammar.
** The Sumerian Question.

the Babylonian priests as a liturgical language and therefore was learned in the religious seminaries as a dead language—a "Church Latin of the ancient Orient," as it were. For this reason, even the Babylonians composed various linguistic aids to help the student priests learn this extinct language; they compiled lists of rare phonetic values occurring in Sumerian, also grammatical paradigms and dictionaries, and, above all, they recorded numerous religious texts, hymns to deities and incantations, with their line-by-line translations in Babylonian. These study aids were the chief guides of the modern scholars to a gradual insight into the structure of this difficult and peculiar language, and if it had not been for them, we would probably still be completely baffled by the Sumerian tongue. Up to World War I, in fact, these bilingual texts with their often imperfect, school-boyish Sumerian were the only understood specimens of that language. Only the pioneering translation by Thureau-Dangin of the monolingual Old Sumerian royal inscriptions of Gudea and other such records* and Poebel's Sumerian Grammar** did gradually pave the road to an understanding of the ancient monolingual texts, too, in the interpretation of which Falkenstein is most outstanding at this time.

(j) *The Interpretation of Hittite and of Cognate Languages of Asia Minor*

The 20th century brought along, in addition to the better comprehension of Sumerian, also the re-discovery of Hittite, a language once spoken in eastern Asia Minor. In 1906, Hugo Winkler discovered the state archives of the Hittite kings in the ruins of Boğazköy, 94 miles east of Ankara; the records preserved there were written on clay tablets, in Babylonian

* *Die sumerischen und akkadischen Königsinschriften*, Leipzig 1907; *Vorderasiatische Bibliothek*, Vol. 1, Part 1.

** *Sumerische Grammatik*. Rostock 1923.

cuneiform writing, but only a small part of them were in the Akkadian language, for their great majority were in Hittite. This find held out the hope for a translation of the Hittite language—or rather, of the *Hittite language of cuneiform literature*, because (as mentioned on page 47 and as it will be discussed on pages 71 *et seq.*) there are inscriptions in "Hittite" hieroglyphics, too.

At the time when World War I broke out, Friedrich Hrozný, a Czech scholar then teaching in Vienna, was busily preparing copies of the Hittite cuneiform records appearing on the clay tablets kept in the museum of Istanbul, commissioned for this work by the *Deutsche Orient-Gesellschaft*, and in the course of this activity he succeeded amazingly quickly in gaining an insight also into the language which, to his greatest amazement, he found to be of an *Indo-European* structure. Also the Hittite records written in cuneiform characters presented solely a problem of linguistic interpretation, but no problem of deciphering the script, and for this reason the word "decipherment"—a term that should be reserved for the re-discovery of the lost key to forgotten scripts—should be avoided when referring to this language, and only the expression "translation," or "interpretation," should be used. In other words, the Hittite texts were to the cuneiform palaeographers as a Hungarian, Finnish or Turkish text written in legible but untranslated Latin script would be to most Europeans today, and by no means did they represent to them the same enigma which a Chinese or Japanese text with its alien script *and* alien language would represent to a European layman.

How was it possible to regain, within relatively so few years, the knowledge of this language, dead and lost for millennia? At first, there was no bilingual, Hittite and Akkadian, text available; only later were a few such texts discovered, and then they were merely instrumental in confirming the already established translations of a few words. Higher hopes were attached at first to a number of *fragments of dictionaries* also discovered in Boğazköy, consisting of word lists of the type already known from Babylonia, listing Sumerian words with their Akkadian equivalents, but completed by the Hittites by a third column showing the translations in their own tongue. These hopes were only partly realized because these dictionaries indicate mostly the meanings of rare words which occur but seldom in the texts, whereas they are mostly useless with respect to every-day vocables especially necessary for a first idea. Moreover, the dictionaries furnish very scant information as to the grammatical structure of the Hittite language.

The principal work was thus to be done by combinatory research on continuous, contextually coherent Hittite texts. The most reliable means for building up an understanding of the contents of such records consisted in the peculiar method of *ideographic writing*, quite characteristic of the Hittite language. The Babylonians and Assyrians already had written their languages partly phonetically, partly with non-phonetic ideograms, partly also mixing the two classes of symbols, writing the stem of the word by an ideogram and the endings phonetically. The Hittites took over this custom, and they added also a characteristic feature of their own, namely that they interspersed also phonetically written Akkadian words and entire groups of words in the Hittite text. Whether these words and groups of words were also pronounced in Akkadian or perhaps in Hittite, is still undecided. At any rate, a *written* Hittite text always contains constituent elements taken from three languages: Sumerian ideograms, many of them with Hittite (or also Akkadian) flexional endings, Akkadian words and word groups, and finally phonetically written Hittite words. As an illustration, I quote here Article 11 of the Hittite laws, transliterated in Latin characters, followed by its English translation. The use of lowercase italics in the transliteration indicates that the word or part of a word appears written phonetically in Hittite, whereas roman capitals indicate a Sumerian ideogram, and italicized capitals an Akkadian word or part of a word:

ták-ku LÚ.ULÙ^{LU} *EL.LUM QA.AZ.ZU na-aš-ma* GÌR-*ŠU ku-iš-ki tu-wa-ar-ni-iz-zi nu-uš-še* 20 GÍN KUBABBAR *pa-a-i.*

"If somebody breaks a free man's hand or leg, he gives him (as a penalty) 20 shekels of silver."

The stem of the word meaning "man" is written here by the Sumerian ideogram LÚ.ULÙ^{LU} to which the phonetic Hittite *-an* ending of the accusative case is added; EL.LUM, "free," is written in Akkadian, and so is QA.AZ.ZU, "his hand," whereas in the word GIR-ŠU, "his leg," the stem is written by the Sumerian ideogram GÌR, and the ending by the Akkadian possessive suffix, -ŠU, "his." The amount of the penalty, 20 GÍN KUBABBAR, "20 shekels of silver," is written in pure Sumerian, and the words *takku* ("if"), *našma* ("or"), *kuiški* ("somebody"), *tuwarnizzi* ("he breaks"), *nu-šše* ("now to him") and *pāi* ("he gives") are written phonetically in Hittite.

In observing texts which have been preserved in several copies, like the Hittite laws, we find sometimes that a given word appears phonetically written in one, while it is represented in the other version by an ideogram the meaning of which is known and thus helps the interpretation of the phonetically written Hittite equivalent. Thus, Article 15 of the laws appears in one copy as *ták-ku* LÚ.ULÙ^{LU}*-aš* EL.LAM *iš-ta-ma-na-aš-ša-an ku-iš-ki iš-kal-la-a-ri* 12 GÍN KUBABBAR *pa-a-i,* whereas in the duplicate *ištamanaššan* is replaced by GEŠTU-*an* ("ear"), so that the translation is: "If somebody slashes a free man's ear, he gives 12 shekels of silver." The word for "not" is written in one copy of the laws in Akkadian, Ú.UL, whereas in another copy it appears in Hittite, as *na-at-ta*.

Occasionally, the ideographic symbols and Akkadian signs may be so predominant in a sentence that the meaning of the entire sentence can be determined on their basis and also the lexical meanings and grammatical functions of the Hittite forms appearing among them can be ascertained. This is illustrated by the following example, taken from the description of a religious festivity:

2 DUMU É.GAL *A.NA* LUGAL SAL.LUGAL *ME.E QA.TI pí-e-da-an-zi* LUGAL SAL.LUGAL ŠU ^{MEŠ}-*ŠU.NU ar-ra-an-zi*.

("Two palace officials extend hand-water to the king [and] queen, king [and] queen wash their hands.")

Here the ideographic elements, DUMU É.GAL ("palace official/s/"), LUGAL ("king") and SAL.LUGAL ("queen"), the Akkadian words ANA ("to," used as the sign of the dative case) and ME.E QA.TI ("water of the hand"), as well as the mixed ideographic-Akkadian ŠU^{MES}-ŠU.NU ("their /-SU.NU in Akkadian/ hands /SU^{MES}/") are clear and help also in the interpretation of the two verbal forms appearing in phonetic Hittite characters, *pedanzi* ("they extend") and *arranzi* ("they wash"), both of which are identified as present tense, third person plural, by the ending *-anzi*.

The consistent utilization of the semi-ideographic method of writing (ideographic word stem and phonetically written ending) furnished first of all the possibility to determine which endings belong to the noun and which to the verb, and in what functions. LUGAL-*uš* ("the king"), LUGAL-*un* ("the king," used as direct object), SAL.LUGAL-*ri* ("to the queen"), etc., contain declensional endings, whereas the endings appearing in GUL-*un* [GUL-*aḫḫun*] ("I struck"), DÙ-*at* ("he made"), etc., are conjugational suffixes. The system of ideography was useful above all in the laws which by their very division into short sentences of the "if some one does such and such a thing, he shall pay such and such a penalty" type restricted the range of possible meanings very narrowly and often, when they contained a sufficiently great number of ideographs, became fully interpretable. This was why Hrozný used the laws as the basic texts for working out the first grammatical and lexical picture of the Hittite language.

One must bear in mind in this connection that while the uniform, systematically recurring representation by ideographs of the most frequently used words will readily reveal the *meaning* of such a word to the decipherer, it will still leave the *spoken form* of that word a secret, until and unless some fortunate accident gives a clue to it. We are, however, still ignorant of the spoken form of just such common, everyday words, many of them important also for comparative Indo-European philology, like *son, brother, sister, wife, horse, dog*, etc., for the very reason that they were always written by ideograms.

The meanings of a number of Hittite words and the most important grammatical functions of the language were thus determined relatively quickly by the *combinatory* method, i.e., by logical conclusions based on the relationship of the words to the rest of the sentence. And as long as Hrozný used solely the combinatory method, he obtained indisputable, lasting results. Encouraged, however, by the results accomplished in the Akkadian field (cf. p. 58) by the *etymological* method, the interpretation of meanings based on the identity or similarity of the spoken forms of words, Hrozný then felt that he was justified in applying the same method to the Hittite language as well, i.e., in deducing the meanings of unknown Hittite words from words of identical pronunciation in other Indo-European tongues. The ease with which this method may creep into combinatory research is well illustrated by the following example:

The sentence *nu* NINDA-*an e-iz-za-at-te-ni wa-a-tar-ma e-ku-ut-te-ni* means "Now you eat bread; water, however, you drink."

In this sentence, the ideogram NINDA, for "bread," was positively identified, and it was logical to assume that the verb governing "bread" as its direct object meant "to eat," although this judgment might have been influenced subtly also by the Indo-European etymology with the New High German *essen*, the Latin *edere*, etc. Bearing in mind the well known *parallelismus membrorum* of the ancient Oriental languages, Hrozný correctly deduced that the second half of the phrase, linked to the first one by *-ma*, meant "water, however, you drink"; yet the sound of the noun *wa-a-tar*, identical with the pronunciation of the Germanic *watar*, "water," another etymologically correct conclusion, is a factor in this instance, too. Now then, the method of judging by such identical spoken forms, without any objective substantiation, implies the great danger that the interpreter will be misled by false identities of sound once in a while. This is what happened repeatedly to Hrozný, too. Thus, he translated the verbal root *dā* as "give," because of the spoken sound which was identical with the sound of the stem of the Latin verb *dare*, whereas later combinatory research determined that its meaning was the very opposite—"take." The word *appa* means "back," but thinking of the Greek *apó*, he translated it as "away"; he translated *piran* ("in front") as "around" because it sounded like the Greek *perí*, the noun *arkuwar* ("prayer"), on the analogy of the Latin *arcere*, as "defense," interpreted *nāwi* ("not yet") as "new," and so on and so forth.

Thus, Hrozný's combinatory researches—fundamental as such, and also correct in many an instance—do contain many an element of uncertainty because of the infiltration of the etymological method, and the young discipline of Hittitology might have gotten on the wrong track if F. Sommer had not pointed, in his monograph entitled *Hethitisches,** temperamentally at the impending dangers and had not steered the research back onto strongly combinatory paths. The authority of Sommer, supported by several younger researchers, must be given the credit for the fact that the new discipline developed into a strict and secure philology within a few years.

There is not much that can be said as yet with respect to the linguistic neighbors of the Hittite tongue in Asia Minor. The non-Indo-European *Proto-Hattian*—the language of the original inhabitants of Ḫatti (Khatti), the characteristic feature of which is a flexion operating chiefly with *prefixes,* instead of suffixes—was perpetuated by the Hittites as the ritual language of the most important state deities, like the Sumerian language in Babylonia, and therefore the student priests had to learn it in school as a dead language. For this reason, the Hittites provided many Proto-Hattian texts with Hittite translations, and these bilingual texts offer to modern research the opportunity to make a headway, step by step at least, into this strange language, while monolingual Proto-Hattian texts are still as good as unintelligible to us for the time being. In Fig. 36 I quote a few sentences from the best known Proto-Hattian-Hittite bilingual text, an adjuration spoken at the laying of a new cross-bar in the palace. The reader might use these sentences to test his own translating ability, but I present here at least a brief summary of the most important word equivalents:

* Leipzig, 1920; Boğazköy Studies, No. 4.

[PROTO-HATTIAN]—

(II 40) *wa-aš-ḫa-ab-ma eš-wu-ur aš-ka-aḫ-ḫi-šir šu-ú-wa* (41) ^{URU}*Ḫa-at-tu-uš ti-it-ta-aḫ-zi-la-at šu-ú-wa* (42) *Ta-ba-ar-na ka-a-at-ti ta-ni-wa-aš* = HITTITE (43) DINGIR^{MEŠ} KUR^{MEŠ} ma-ni-ia-aḫ-ḫi-ir da-a-ir-ma-at ^{URU}Ḫa-at-tu-ši (44) šal-li ^{GIŠ}ŠÚ.A da-a-ir-ma-at nu-za La-ba-ar-na-aš LUGAL-u[š e-eš-zi]

"The gods allotted the countries; but for Ḫattuša they took the great throne, but they took it, and Labarna is king."

. . . .

[PROTO-HATTIAN]—

(III 19) *a-an-tu-uḫ li-e-zu-u-uḫ li-eš-te-ra-aḫ ba-la l[i-e-še-ip-še-ip]* (20) *ba-la an-ne-eš ka-a-ḫa-an-wa-šu-id-du-ú-un* = HITTITE. (21) da-a-aš-ma-aš-za TUG$^{ḪI.A}$ ^{KUŠ}GAR.TÁG$^{ḪI.A}$ ^{KUŠ}E.SIR$^{ḪI.A}$-ia (22) na-aš-ša-an da-a-iš ^{GIŠ}DAG-ti

(23) *[a-an-tu-uḫ?] li?-e?-ú-da-ta-nu pa-la li-e-iz-zi-bi-ir* (24) *pa-la [an-ne]-eš ka-a-ḫa-an-wa-šu-id-du-un* = HITTITE. (25) [da]-a-aš?-[ma-z]a GA?.KIN.AG? *IM?.ZU*?-ia na-at-ša-an da-a-iš ^{GIŠ}DAG-ti

"But he took the garments, the drapes (?) and the [the shoe]s and placed them onto the throne.—But he took cheese (?) and rennet (?) and placed it onto the throne."

. . . .

[PROTO-HATTIAN]—

(40) *a-ša-aḫ ta-aš-te-nu-ú-wa bi-e-wi-il* (41) *iš-ga-a-ru ta-aš-te-e-ta-nu-ú-wa* = HITTITE. (42) nu-wa-kán i-da-lu-uš an-da? li-e ú-iz-zi (43) i-da-lu-uš-wa-kán UKU-aš É-ri an-da li-e ú-iz-zi

"And an evil one shall not come in, an evil man shall not come into the house."

. . . .

[PROTO-HATTIAN]—

(51) *ma-al-ḫi-ib-ḫu? te-e-ta-aḫ-šu-ú-ul a-ša-aḫ-bi* (52) *ta-aš-tu-u-ta šu-u-la* ^{d}*Šu-li-in-kat-ti ka-at-ti* (53) *ta-ni-wa-aš ú-un-ḫu-bi* = HITTITE. (54) na-aš-ta a-aš-šu an-da tar-ni-eš-ki-id-du (55) i-da-lu-ma-kán an-da li-e tar-na-a-i (58) ^{d}Šu-li-in-kat-ti-iš-ša-an LUGAL-uš an-da e-eš-zi

"Then he shall let in the good one, but the evil one he shall not let in; King Šulinkatti is inside."

FIG. 36. From a bilingual Proto-Hattian-Hittite text. (*Keilschrifturkunden aus Boğhazköi*, Vol. II, No. 2, column II, lines 40–44; column III, lines 19–25, 40–44, 51–56.

wašḫab-ma = Hittite DINGIR^{MEŠ} = "gods"
ešwur = Hittite KUR^{MEŠ} = "countries"
aškaḫḫir = Hittite *maniiaḫḫir* = "they allotted"
šuwa probably = Hittite *dāir-ma-at* = "but they took," but it may have another meaning
titaḫzilat = Hittite *šalli* ^{GIŠ}ŠÚ.A = "the great throne"
katti (*katte*) = Hittite LUGAL-*uš* = "king"
taniwaš = Hittite *ešzi* = "there is"
antuḫ = Hittite *dāš-ma-aš-za* = "he took them (-*aš*) however (-*ma*) to himself (-*za*)"
lē-zuḫ = Hittite TÚG$^{\text{ḪI.A}}$ = "garments"
le-šteraḫ = Hittite ^{KUŠ}GAR.TÁG$^{\text{ḪI.A}}$ = "drapes (?)"
bala (*pala*) = Hittite -*ia* and *nu* = "and"
lē-šepšep = Hittite ^{KUŠ}E.SIR$^{\text{ḪI.A}}$ = "shoes"
anneš = Hittite *dāiš* = "he placed"
kā-ḫanwašuiddun = Hittite ^{GIŠ}DAG-*ti* = "onto the chair"
lē-udatanu = Hittite GA.KIN.AG = "cheese"
a-šaḫ = Hittite *idaluš* = "evil"
taš-te-nuwa (*taš-te-ta-nuwa*) = Hittite *ande lē uizzi* = "he shall not come in"
he-uil = Hittite É-*ri* = "into the house"
išgaru = Hittite *idaluš* UKÙ-*aš* = "an evil man, villain"
malḫib = Hittite *aššu* = "good"
te-taḫ-šul = Hittite *anda tarneškiddu* = "he shall always let in"
a-šaḫ-bi = Hittite *idalu-ma* = "but the evil"
taš-tuta šula = Hittite *anda lē tarnai* = "he shall not let in"
unḫubi = Hittite *anda* = "inside"?

Like Hittite, *Luwian* and *Palaian* also are Indo-European languages, yet in these instances, too, caution must be exercised in applying the etymological method. In a few instances, Hittite parallel texts could be found for certain Luwian texts, and thus it was possible to undertake a certain combinatory work on the Luwian language. Fig. 37 presents a sentence from the best known such bilingual texts, where the concordance, by the way, is not quite literal. Luwian texts

Luwian: (22) ^{d}'*Ša-an-ta-aš* LUGAL-*uš* ^{d}*An-na-ru-um-mi-en-zi* (23) *aš-ḫa-nu-wa-an-ta ku-in-zi wa-aš-ša-an-ta-ri* (24) ^{d}*Lu-u-la-ḫi-in-za-aš-tar ḫu-u-up-pa-ra-za ku-in-zi ḫi-iš-ḫi-ia-an-ti* = HITTITE. (I 36) e-ḫu ^{d}*MARDUK* kat-ti-ti-ma-at-ta ^{d}In-na-ra-u-wa-an-ta-aš (37) ú-wa-du e-eš-ḫa-nu-wa-an-ta ku-e-eš ú-e-eš-ša-an-ta (38) LÚ^{MEŠ} Lu-u-la-ḫi-ia-aš-ša-an ḫu-up-ru-uš ku-i-e-eš iš-ḫi-ia-an-ti-iš

(Translation from the Hittite part) "Come, Marduk (= Luwian "King Šanta"), but let with you come the 'robust (?) (gods),' don the blood-stained (clothes), (also) the Lulaḫi (gods) who (are) swathed in . . ."

FIG. 37. From the Luwian-Hittite *Quasibilinguis* (*Keilschrifturkunden aus Boğhazköi*, Vol. IX, No. 31, col. II, lines 22–24 = col. I, lines 36–38).

without Hittite parallels still remain very difficult to handle. As for Palaian, no real possibility of interpreting this language has even been found as yet.

(k) *The Interpretation of Hurrian*

The only Hurrian records heretofore known are monolingual texts, written in Babylonian cuneiform characters. Quite recently, however, a text consisting of a few lines written bilingually in Akkadian and Hurrian was found by the French in Ugarit (Ras Shamrah), and it is expected to be made public in the near future. But it is too short to be likely to help us much, and also the isolated Hurrian words appearing here and there in the Akkadian word-list are of not much practical use. Thus, on the whole we still remain dependent on the combinatory method which involves many more difficulties with respect to the interpretation of Hurrian than in the case of Hittite, because the Hurrians used mainly a phonetic script and rarely employed ideograms. While in the Hittite texts the ideograms reveal the meanings of the words, even though they give no clue as to their pronunciation, the Hurrian records show the spoken form of almost every word, but by doing so, they preclude the possibility of fathoming its meaning.

This is why the religious texts written in the Hurrian language, a great many of which are contained in the Hittite archives of Boğazköy, and some specimens of which, in vowelless Ugaritic script, appear also in the temple library of Ugarit, are still as good as unintelligible, except for the meanings of a few words which Carl Georg von Brandenstein has deduced by the combinatory method.

A more favorable aspect is presented by the "*Mitanni Letter*" of King Tušratta (cf. p. 46), discovered in the archives of El Amarna, Egypt, in 1888. Tušratta sent a number of lengthy letters to Egypt, written in Akkadian and containing a great many repetitions, and he sent also a very long communication, containing more than 400 lines, in his native Hurrian tongue. Now then, in any text written in cuneiform characters, the proper names, names of deities, geographic names, etc. are always clearly identified as such by their determinatives, even though the language of the record may be absolutely unknown to the reader. Since the names occurring in the Mitanni Letter are the same ones as appear in the Akkadian letters of Tušratta, it may well be assumed that also the Hurrian letter deals with the same topics as the Akkadian epistles. Thus, soon tolerably intelligible word combinations can be identified, above all in connection with the names, e.g., ^{I}*Ni-im-mu-u-ri-i-aš* KUR *Mi-zi-ir-ri-e-we-ni-eš iw-ri-iš*, meaning "Nimmuria (name of the Pharaoh), king (*iwriš*) of Egypt (KUR *Mizirri*)," or ^{I}*Ar-ta-ta-a-maš am-ma-ti-iw-wu-uš*, meaning "my grandfather, Artatama" (known as such from the Akkadian letters of Tušratta). Let the following examples be cited here for entire short sentences recurring in Akkadian as well as in Hurrian: The Hurrian DINGIR^{MEŠ} *e-e-en-na-šu-uš na-ak-ki-te-en* = the Akkadian *ilāni*^{MEŠ} *li-me-eš-še-ru-šu* = "may the gods will it"; the Hurrian *i-nu-ú-me-e-ni-i-in* ᵈ*Ši-mi-gi tar-šu-an-niš* . . . ta-a-ti-a = the Akkadian *ki-i-me-e a-mi-lu-ú-tum* ᵈ*Šamaš i-ra-'a-am-šu* = "as mankind loves the sun" [Hurrian *inu* = Akkadian *kī* (*-me*) = "as"; Hurrian *taršuanni-* = Akkadian *amīlūtum* = "mankind"; Hurrian *tat-* = Akkadian *ra' amu* = "love"]. The utilization of such opportunities enabled Jensen and Messerschmidt in the late 19th century, and recently also other investigators, to make considerable progress with the aid of the combinatory method in the understanding of the vocabulary and of the quite involved grammatical forms of the outlandish Hurrian language, and to translate at least individual passages of the Mitanni Letter more or less reliably. Yet, although that text has been explored and analyzed for decades, the clearly or at least fairly intelligible parts still alternate with long passages which can be translated with great difficulty only or not at all.

(1) *The Interpretation of Urartaean*

The Urartaeans were younger kinfolk of the Hurrians. They lived in what later became Armenia and left behind them about 180 inscriptions of various lengths (building dedications, votive inscriptions, war reports and individual annal passages), dating from the 9th–7th centuries B.C., written in the Neo-Assyrian cuneiform script, but mostly in the Urartaean language (which certain research linguists prefer to call *Chaldaean*). The relationship of Hurrian and Urartaean is, however, not close enough to permit us to expect any result from the etymological method; the Urartaean language must be interpreted by the combinatory method, without outside references. The first assistance is given to us once again by the names (of persons, of deities, of geographic units) written in combination with certain determinatives, then by the short and clear phrasing of most of the inscriptions, as well as by the not too sparing use of ideograms. In studying inscriptions of very stereotyped contents, one often finds an ideogram in one and phonetic symbols in the corresponding spot in another. Thus many a linguistic fact has been deduced from the monolingual inscriptions by the combinatory method alone. There are also two stelae known which are inscribed bilingually, in Urartaean and Assyrian, viz.: the Kelišin Stela, in the Kelišin Pass on the Iraqi-Iranian border, and the nearby Stela of Topzauae. But only the first-mentioned one has been reported on satisfactorily; it has yielded a number of lexical equivalences as well as a few grammatical facts. But no complete, scientifically incontestable representation of the Stela of Topzauae, much more difficult to read, has been made available as yet.

(m) *The Interpretation of Early Elamite*

A few words are all that can be said about the inscriptions left by the early Elamite kings in Babylonian cuneiform script, dating probably from the 13th and 12th centuries B.C. They must be interpreted chiefly without any outside reference, for there is only one among them to which there exists a very brief Akkadian parallel text. The Early Elamite cuneiform writing contains determinatives, but few ideograms. An important lexical help, however, is provided by the Neo-Elamite translations of the inscriptions of the Achaemenides which reveal the meanings of a number of Elamite words, although still not of sufficiently many to clarify completely the far richer vocabulary and frequently differing grammatical structure of the more ancient language. Elamite was long a stepchild of the research into cuneiform literature, and only in recent years did Hinz make good beginnings with the combinatory interpretation of Early Elamite inscriptions, too.

(n) *The Decipherment of Ugaritic*

Early Elamite closes the sizable list of the languages written in Babylonian cuneiform characters, and all there still remains to be discussed in this connection is the *alphabetic* writing used by the inhabitants of Ugarit, on the northern Syrian coast, in the 15th and 14th centuries B.C. This script was written on clay tablets and resembles the cuneiform writing in appearance at least. It was discovered by French excavators in Ras Shamrah as recently as 1929 and aroused great interest as a new factor come to light in the otherwise thoroughly explored territory of Syria.

The differences between this newly discovered script and the already known Babylonian cuneiform writing was immediately recognized, because this script consisted of a mere 30 characters, all very simple in shape, and there were no determinatives. These features suggested promptly that this was no syllabic writing like the Babylonian cuneiform script, but an *alphabetic* system like the Early Persian writing. The distinct separation of most individual words by vertical strokes seemed to be a help to decipherment, whereas the absence of bilingual texts had to be regarded as an impediment. On the whole, however, the prospects for the decipherment of an alphabetic script are always favorable, because the small number of individual characters restricts the possible interpretations to a much narrower range than the one to be considered in the case of a syllabic writing which employs a hundred or more different symbols.

The separation of the words was a great help in the study of the morphology, and since the latter seemed to indicate that the language was a Semitic one, Hans Bauer, the Semitist of Halle, felt justified, in April 1930, in tentatively assigning Semitic consonantal values to the characters constituting the undeciphered words. This attempt at reading the words as if they belonged to a Semitic language was just one of various possibilities, for the newly discovered script in itself might have suggested quite different languages as well. But Bauer was lucky: The language was actually Semitic, and he had interpreted 17 characters correctly. In the meantime, also the Frenchmen Dhorme and Virolleaud attacked the problem, and by the following year the value of each and every character of the Ugaritic alphabet was determined correctly, without any bilingual text whatsoever and without any outside reference at all, solely on the ground of the assumption that the language in question was of a Semitic structure. Let it be mentioned that also the inscriptions appearing on several bronze axes played a part in Bauer's decipherment. These inscriptions appeared in a shorter form, consisting of only six symbols which Bauer assumed to be simply the name of the owner, and in a longer version which contained four other symbols before those six. Bauer suspected that these four symbols represented the word for "axe," which in Hebrew is *garzen*, written by the four consonants *grzn*, whereas the corresponding word in the cognate Ugaritic language is, as it was established later, *ḫrṣn* (cf. Fig. 38). The Ugaritic consonantal alphabet is shown in Fig. 30.

The accuracy of the consonantal values deduced by Bauer, Dhorme and Virolleaud was soon corroborated by various facts. The first and most immediate one of these confirming facts was that the soon published long texts, even though still obscure in many particulars, turned out to contain generally well intelligible mythological tales in the Ugaritic language, still an unknown tongue and yet related to the Semitic languages. Moreover, the assignment of those values to the various characters yielded also a number of Hurrian names of deities which had not been sought in the texts and yet, once identified, formed a closed circle. And finally, later discoveries of Akkadian and Ugaritic lists of names of cities, etc. furnished a further confirmation of the correctness of the consonantal values deduced. These lists are not bilingual, they do not contain identical lists in two languages. They are *monolingual* lists, some in Babylonian cuneiform script, others in Ugaritic cuneiform characters, enumerating the inhabited places of the land of Ugarit *in a strongly varying*

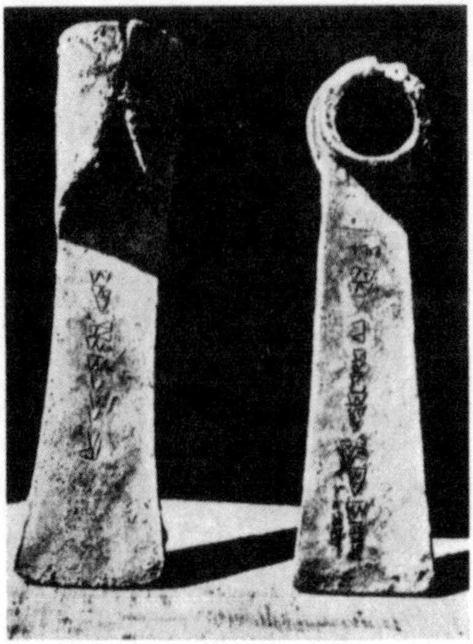

Fig. 38. Ugaritic axes with inscriptions. (From Friedrich, *Ras Schamra*, Fig. 4.)

order. Thus, even if the name of a town appears in a certain place on a tablet bearing inscriptions in Akkadian, it cannot be expected to occur in the corresponding place on an Ugaritic tablet. They would hardly have offered a point of departure to the first decipherers, but they help us today better to understand the phonetic structure of Ugaritic by equating the Babylonian ^{alu}*Iz-pi* with the Ugaritic *Hzp*, the

Babylonian ^{alu}*Ba-aq-at* with the Ugaritic *Bq't*, the Babylonian ^{alu}*Ja-ku*-SIG$_5$ with the Ugaritic *Jkn'm*, etc. (SIG$_5$ is an ideogram for "good," and also the Ugaritic *n'm* means "good").

I would not want to withhold a proof of the correct reading and translation of the figures from my readers. A similar list enumerates towns and villages and their deliveries of wine, indicating the numbers of the jugs delivered, and the numbers are written *phonetically in* Ugaritic. The sum total of these numbers is 148, and the list actually ends with the expression, written *in Akkadian and using numerals*, "1 *me-at* 48 DUG GEŠTIN" = "148 jugs of wine." Thus, we may feel absolute confidence in the rapidly accomplished decipherment of the Ugaritic script, too.

3. The Hittite Hieroglyphic Writing

The late 19th century regarded the Hittite hieroglyphic writing as the third great problem in the field of ancient Oriental scripts, ranking as such with the Egyptian hieroglyphics and the cuneiform writing. A different view is being taken nowadays. The plethora of texts written in cuneiform script has revealed to us so much about the races and language of eastern Asia Minor and northern Syria that the not very numerous Hittite hieroglyphic inscriptions with their not too significant contents appear somewhat pallid next to them; as a matter of fact, they are just a late, weak offshoot of Hittite civilization. But, nevertheless, these inscriptions permit us to form an ever clearer idea of still another Indo-European language beside cuneiform Hittite, Luwian and Palaian, and moreover, the problem of the *decipherment* of hieroglyphic Hittite still remains an interesting one. For in 1930, after six decades of futile efforts, finally a practicable method was found to achieve a combinatory decipherment without a bilingual text, and the later discovery of a large bilingual text confirmed and expanded the results obtained previously. Thus, in the case of the Hittite hieroglyphs there exists actually the possibility of checking up on the ability of the decipherer.

(a) *General Facts*

Monuments bearing inscriptions in Hittite hieroglyphics have been known since the middle of the 19th century A.D., especially those found in eastern Asia Minor, on and about the soil of the ancient Hittite empire, as well as in the adjacent part of northern Syria, above all in the important city of Karkhemish at the bend of the Euphrates. The writing used in these inscriptions is primarily a *monumental* writing, but it appears also on *seals*. Monuments bearing inscriptions in hieroglyphics and seals with cuneiform and hieroglyphic characters are known to us from as early as the era of the Hittite empire (between 1400 and 1200 B.C.). On the other hand, the major part of the North Syrian inscriptions are of more recent origin; they date from the 10th–8th centuries B.C. With the gradual absorption of Syria in the As-

FIG. 39. Hieroglyphic Hittite inscriptions from Karkhemish. (From Friedrich, *Entzifferungsgeschichte der hethitischen Hieroglyphenschrift*, Fig. 2.)

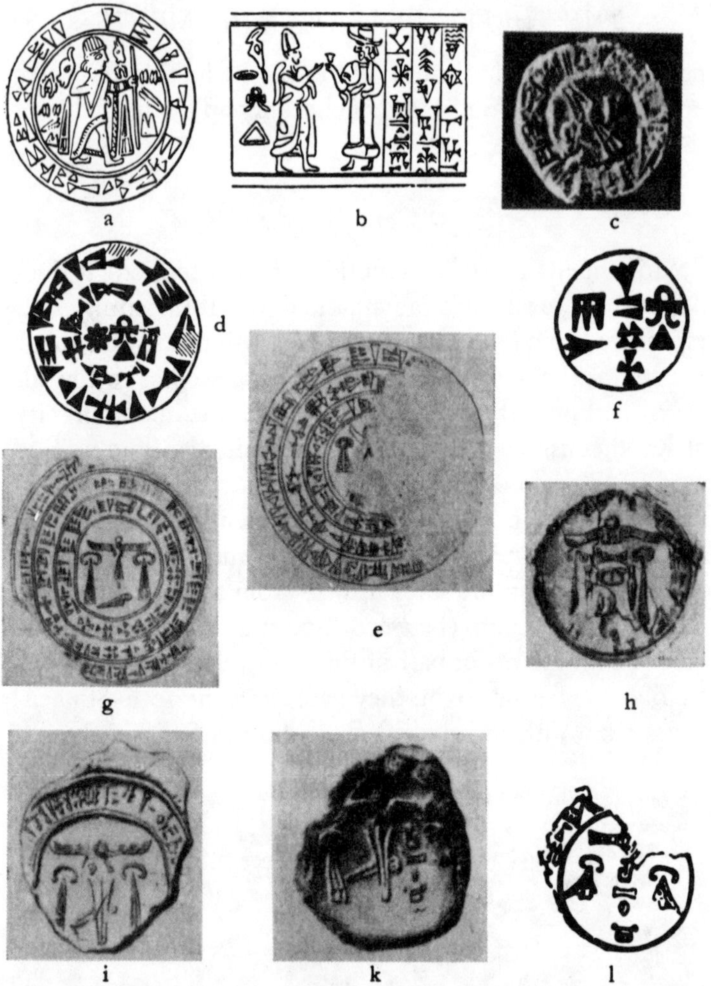

FIG. 40. Seals with cuneiform-hieroglyphic Hittite inscriptions. (From Friedrich, *Entzifferungsgeschichte der hethitischen Hieroglyphenschrift*, Fig. 5.)

(*a*) Tarkummuwa of Mirā. (*b*) Indilumma. (*c*) Išputaḫšu of Kizwatna. (*d*) Tabarna of Ḫatti. (*e*) Arnuwanda of Ḫatti. (*f*) So-called Ziti seal. (*g*) Urḫi-Tešup of Ḫatti. (*h*) Šuppiluliuma of Ḫatti. (*i*) Ḫattušili of Ḫatti. (*k*) Ḫattušili and his wife, Puduḫepa. (*l*) Queen Puduḫepa of Ḫatti.

syrian empire, the hieroglyphic writing disappeared about 700 B.C. A hieroglyphic Hittite inscription, from Karkhemish, appears in Fig. 39, whereas Fig. 40 shows several cuneiform-hieroglyphic seals.

A special comment is necessary with respect to the *foils of lead* found in Assur, probably brought there from somewhere else, which are inscribed with a very cursive hieroglyphic writing. Contemporary research considers them letters; the fact that they were found, rolled up, in the foundations of a house is probably attributable to a mistake of the builder who erroneously regarded them as having magic powers. Also the cursive form of writing suggests ordinary, every-day contents. It seems therefore that this writing was used on monuments in an elaborate, pictorial form (occasionally, however, also with cursive forms) and in daily life in a strongly cursive variety, analogously to the situation in Egypt where both the hieroglyphic writing of the monuments and the cursive hieratic and demotic scripts of ordinary daily life remained in use side by side.

The designation *"Hittite" hieroglyphics* was introduced by the British research philologist Sayce, shortly after 1870. Egypt and Babylonia-Assyria were practically the only two nations of the ancient Orient known to the philologists of those days as two culturally and scripturally clearly distinct entities, and the newly discovered script on monuments of a likewise distinct art appeared as the legacy of a third civilized race of the Orient of remote antiquity. Both Egyptian and cuneiform records had made reference to a land and people named Ḫatti (or Khatti) in northern Syria, and the Hittites are mentioned occasionally in the Old Testament, too. This was the reason why Sayce regarded these monuments as works of the Hittites, and he considered them at first a Semitic race. The situation was clarified only by the discovery of the Hittite archive of Boğazköy which revealed the Hittite language to be an *Indo-European* tongue, even though written in cuneiform characters. There arose then, however, the question as to the closer relationship of *cuneiform Hittite* and *hieroglyphic Hittite*, which still has not been answered completely. The two languages are indubitably closely related but by no means identical. In fact, hieroglyphic Hittite shows features closely related to Luwian. But when answering this question, we must bear in mind that all the lengthier hieroglyphic inscriptions date from the last eras of hieroglyphic writing, and that our only relics of the Hittite empire and cuneiform Hittite still consist merely of a few brief and linguistically barren inscriptions.

(b) *The Basic Principles of the Hieroglyphic Script and the Possibility of a Decipherment*

As we know today, the Hittite hieroglyphic writing also consists of the same three elements as the Egyptian writing and the Babylonian cuneiform script, viz.: word-signs (ideograms), phonetic symbols, and determinatives, some of the latter prefixed and some suffixed to the word which they qualify. The important fact is that the phonetic symbols, unlike the Egyptian symbols, but analogous to the cuneiform characters, represent clearly distinct syllables, indicating the vowels. The individual words are often (but unfortunately, not systematically) separated from each other by the separation mark IC. The characteristic features of the word-signs consist in their carefully drawn pictorial shapes, their relatively rarer occurrence, and their position at the beginning of the words. Simpler and often cursive symbols occur very frequently, chiefly in the second half of a word *after* such pictograms; they may be regarded as the phonetic (syllabic) elements. Since in a pictographic script the word-signs are mostly directly understandable as pictures, they may well be expected to furnish clues as to the meanings of the words and the grammatical (nominal or verbal) functions of the endings. Let it be pointed out, though, that in the Hittite hieroglyphics the pictorial character of the symbols often became indistinct as a result of the conventionalization of their shapes. Who would expect, for instance, the symbols shown in Fig. 41 to stand for "house," "sun" and "god,"

FIG. 41. Hittite hieroglyphic symbols for "House," "Sun" and "God."

respectively? As in the cuneiform script, also in the Hittite hieroglyphic writing, the determinative of names of deities is identical with the pictorially unclear ideogram of "god." Ten persons are referred to by name on the family relief of Karkhemish, and each name is introduced by a small, oblique stroke, the determinative for persons which resembles the vertical wedge appearing before the names of male persons in the Babylonian cuneiform writing and seems to have been created in imitation of the latter.

The *direction of the writing* is made evident by two clues: First, the picture of a person pointing at himself, appearing at the beginning of the inscriptions and meaning "I (am)" (cf. Fig. 42), and secondly, the unfilled portion of the last

FIG. 42. The Egyptian and hieroglyphic Hittite pictograms for the pronoun "I."

line of many an inscription (cf. Fig 39). It is evident also that, as in the Egyptian writing, the heads of all human animal figures are turned as if they were looking toward the beginning of the line, the hands are stretched in that direction, and also most of the feet appear to be walking that way. Moreover, the writing alternates in direction from line to line, in other words its direction is *boustrophedon* (a Greek expression which means literally "as the ox turns" and is generally used as a technical term to designate this regularly alternating direction of writing, as an allusion to the direction in which teams of oxen walk when ploughing a field).

Particular difficulties were presented by the definition of *syllabic phonetic values*. The first students of the script had practically no bilingual texts available to enable them to identify names as such; the two cuneiformly-and-hieroglyphically inscribed seals of Tarkummuwa and Indilumma (Figs. 40-a and 43) contained so many obscurities even in the cuneiform portions that they did more to mislead than to clarify matters. The researchers thus were forced to look for other clues.

Now then, it could be safely assumed on the analogy of other inscriptions of the ancient Orient that the royal authors began also these records by stating their names and titles and designating themselves as the king of such and such land or city. Sayce had already identified the ideo-

Tarku-muwa KING *Me+ra-á* LAND
"Tarkummuwa, king of the land of Mera"

FIG. 43. Text of the Tarkummuwa seal.

grams for "king" and "land" on the basis of the bilingual Tarkummuwa seal (Fig. 43), and these helped now to analyze also the initial portions of other inscriptions into "I

(a) *Kar-ka-me*^{CITY}
(b) *Tu-wa-nu-wa*^{CITY}
(c) *Ku+r(a)-ku-ma*^{CITY}
(d) *A-ma-tu*^{LAND}

FIG. 44. Hieroglyphic Hittite writing of the geographic names Karkhemish, Tuwanuwa, Gurguma and Ḥamāt.

/am/ X (*a name written phonetically*), king of the land or of the city /of/ Y." And in fact, in the many inscriptions found in Karkhemish, for instance, all those places where names of lands or cities were expected to appear showed always the sequence of symbols shown in Fig. 44, followed by the determinative ("city") or ("land"). This group of symbols could therefore be suspected of being the name of Karkhemish. The corresponding places in the inscriptions from Tyana (*Tu-wa-nu-wa* in cuneiform Hittite), *Mar'aš* (*Gur-gu-ma* in cuneiform Hittite) and Hamāt were always occupied by the respective groups of symbols shown in Fig. 44. I have deliberately selected mutually confirmatory examples: *Tuwanuwa* contains the syllable *wa* twice, *Gurguma* contains *gu* twice (in the first instance with an *r*), the syllable *tu* appears in *Tu-wa-nu-wa* and in *A-ma-tu*, *ma* in *A-ma-tu* and *Gur-gu-ma*. This method permits the identification of geographic names and, from those, of syllabic signs with a convincing assurance, without any bilingual text such as Champollion had, and without the knowledge of any list of monarchs, such as Grotefend had available.

Names of the monarchs of the "hieroglyphic Hittites" were not as well known to the decipherers as had been the names of Persian rulers to Grotefend, but the Assyrian kings had recorded the names of a few North Syrian kings in their reports in cuneiform script on their military campaigns against North Syria. If the exact era of such a king was known and a hieroglyphic inscription from his city could be determined archaeologically to originate from the same era, there existed under certain circumstances a certain degree of probability of deducing also the correct reading of the names of "hieroglyphic Hittite" monarchs. This was how a *Mu-wa-ta-li* of Gurguma, an *Ur-ḫi-li-nu* of Hamāt and a *Wa-r-pa-la-wa* of Tuwanuwa were re-discovered in the inscriptions (Fig. 45).

(a) *Mu-wa-ta-li*, (b) *U+r(a)-ḫi-li-na*, (c) *Wa+r(a)-pa-la-wa*

FIG. 45. Hieroglyphic Hittite writing of the names of the monarchs Muwatali, Urḫilinu and Warpalawa.

(c) *The Progress of the Decipherment*

With my discussion of the possibilities of a decipherment, I began, unawares as it were, to report on the course of the decipherment itself and have already mentioned some of the results of the research. Of course, these results were not obtained as easily as they seem to be to some one who is in the position to survey the whole matter after the conclusion of the progress and development. The progress of the research was much more complicated and controversial, and the earlier investigators in particular did not proceed along the lines of sufficiently clear and sharp logical considerations. On the other hand, though, they had to work with far fewer inscriptions than the later analysts and our own contemporaries. Thus the interpretation of those very inscriptions was a very painstaking process which involved many a blind alley; we may say, in fact, that for sixty long years, from 1870 to 1930, everything in this domain was vague and uncertain. A report on all those uncertainties seems to be uncalled for today, when we finally stand on a firm foundation. Those who wish to know the state of affairs just before the outbreak of World War II are referred to the author's *Entzifferungsgeschichte der hethitischen Hieroglyphenschrift.** In the present book, I shall list merely some of the most important positive results.

We owe a debt of gratitude to Sayce, the first investigator,

* "History of the Decipherment of the Hittite Hieroglyphic Writing." (Stuttgart, 1939; special issue No. 3 of *Welt als Geschichte.*)

for the recognition of the meanings of the ideograms for "king," "city," "land" and "god," as well as of the symbol  as the ending of the nominative case (*s*) and of  as the ending of the accusative (*n*). Observing that all designations of deities began with the ideogram for "god," he concluded correctly also that this ideogram was used as a determinative before names of deities as well. These correct interpretations, however, are buried under a vast number of fanciful and wrong decipherments and translations. Ménant was the first man to recognize correctly (about 1890) that the picture of the person pointing at himself which appears at the beginning of the inscriptions has the same meaning as the Egyptian hieroglyphic depicting a person pointing at himself, i.e., *I* (cf. Fig. 42), and that the first symbols of the inscriptions are to be translated, analogously with many other ancient Oriental inscriptions, as "I /am/ X."

The most comprehensive, but at the same time also most difficult and most controversial attempt at a decipherment and interpretation in the early era of this research was undertaken by Jensen in 1894. He identified the name of the city of Karkhemish correctly, but his subsequent determination of the phonetic values of many symbols—some of which he regarded, quite unsystematically, as representing individual consonants and vowels, others as open and closed syllables, still others as symbols for more involved groups of sounds or ideograms—was so arbitrary that his findings were disputed even then, not even to mention his opinion that the hieroglyphic inscriptions contained the Indo-European Armenian language in the same form in which it was handed down to us in the literature dating from the Christian era. Thus, the work of Jensen actually aroused distrust in the decipherments, and today, when the decipherment finally rests on a firm foundation, we may disregard without com-

The Kings and Queens of the New Empire

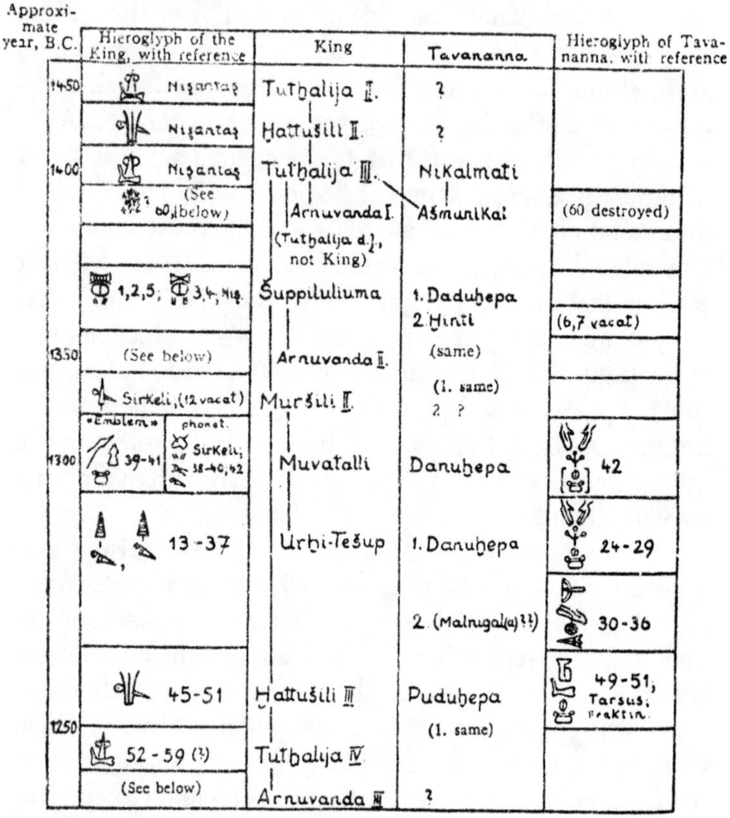

Fig. 46. Hieroglyphics representing the names of great Hittite kings and queens. (From Güterbock, *Siegel aus Bogazköy* I, p. 61.)

ment his first attempt in 1894, as well as his later opinion that the inscriptions consisted of mere conglomerations of ideographically written royal titles, not only without any historical data but even without indicating the name of any person or geographic entity. Jensen's attempt at decipherment was, unfortunately, a useless waste of a great deal of energy. But also Thompson, Cowley and Carl Frank, who attempted a decipherment just before and shortly after World War I, failed to achieve any convincing result.

Meriggi, Gelb, Forrer and Bossert were the ones who brought the whole undertaking onto more solid soil, about 1930. The Italian Meriggi succeeded in identifying an ideogram meaning "son," and thus a genealogy which proved useful in the reading of the names of the monarchs. One of the words identified by Gelb was the verb meaning "to make," the correctly transliterated form of which, *aia-*, became a factor of importance in the correct classification of the language of the hieroglyphic texts as cognate with Luwian. Forrer's recognition of a *formula of imprecation* was fundamental for the analysis of the sentence structure. Bossert discovered the proper reading of the royal name *Warpalawa* and of the name *Kupapa*, the name of an often mentioned goddess. All the investigators named here operate with geographic names and names of persons, as those discussed above. It is difficult to appraise the independent contribution of Hrozný, already known to the reader as the successful first investigator of cuneiform Hittite, who also began to work on hieroglyphic Hittite in 1932.

In the years 1933–1937, also the number of cuneiform Hittite *seals from Boğazköy* increased gratifyingly, and the investigators learned from them the hieroglyphic Hittite written forms of the names of most great Hittite kings (Fig. 46), although most of them in ideographic form, for *Mu-ta-li* = *Mu*(*wa*)*ttalli* was the only one written syllabically. But at least the names of the queens *Puduḫepa* and *Tanuḫepa* were written likewise with syllabic signs and yielded the phonetic values of a few more syllabic symbols, and they were helpful also in establishing the reading of the name of the chief goddess of the Hittite mountain shrine of Yazilikaya, ^{d}***Ḫa-ba-tu*** = the cuneiform ^{d}***Ḫé-bat*** (Fig. 47).

^{d}*Ḫa-ba-tu*

FIG. 47. Hieroglyphic Hittite version of the name of the goddess Ḫebat.

Thus, to sum it all up, at the time when World War II broke out, the *reading* of a great many syllabic signs seemed to be certain or very probable, and we had a fair idea about the *inflexion* of hieroglyphic Hittite, too, on the basis of the lengthier inscriptions of later dates. The *lexical* research, though, was still encumbered with many uncertainties, above all also because of the not all too great number and slight variations in text of the hieroglyphic Hittite inscriptions. Thus even the translations already supplied by Meriggi and Hrozný for most of the inscriptions had to be regarded with reservations, and in Hrozný's translations in particular some more question marks had to be added to the many already appearing in them. The Indo-European character of the language was only very vaguely recognizable.

The fall of 1947 then brought a big, electrifying surprise: Bossert found several long inscriptions on the hill called Karatepe in eastern Cilicia, which were partly in hieroglyphic Hittite and partly in Phoenician and dated from the late part of the 8th century B.C. They soon turned out to be bilingual records. As of this date, the almost intact Phoenician inscriptions, totalling about sixty lines, have been published completely, but the just fragmentarily preserved hieroglyphic Hittite texts only partly, and even so not in their original form but as they were schematically copied by Bossert, so that there remain a few uncertainties concerning the sequence of the symbols. It is therefore not yet possible to reach any conclusive judgment, but the extraordinary signifi-

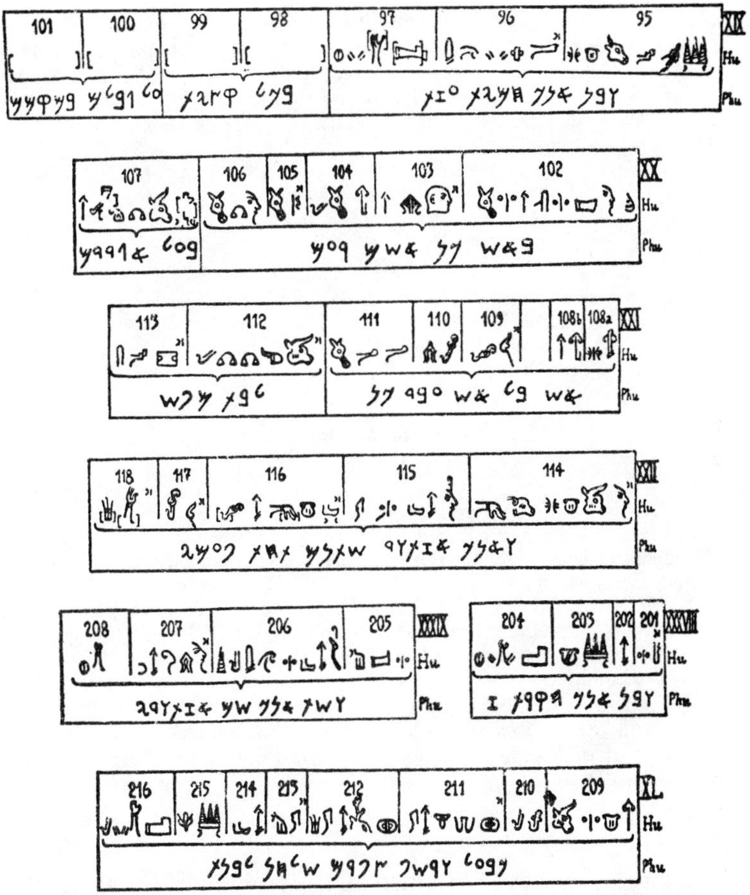

FIG. 48. Sentences XIX–XXII and XXXVIII–XL of the bilingual text of Karatepe. (Bossert, Archiv Orientálni XVIII, 3, pp. 24–25, and Bossert, *Jahrbuch für kleinasiatische Forschung* I, p. 272.)

cance of the bilingual texts is obvious even so. We see to our great satisfaction that the determination by the combinatory method of the readings and grammatical forms, as worked out by the above-named investigators in the 1930's, was correct in every essential point, and also a great many of the

Hieroglyphic Hittite:

XIX. FORT ḫa+r(a)-ná-si-pa-wá "ARM li-mi-tá-ā BUILD? tū-mi-ḫa (rest destroyed) XX. IDEOGR. á-tu-wa-a+r(a)-i-wa-ta "HEAD -tí-i kwa?-ta-n(u) "á-ta á-s.-ta "?-u-s.-?-?-i XXI. kwa?-wa kwa?-i "DOWN-n(u) nu-ti tà?-ta "mu-ka-s.-s.-n(u) "HOUSE-na-a XXII. "á-mu-pa-wá-ma-tá ă-śi-ī-da-wa+ra-ś. "FOOT-pa-tá-ī-n(u) "DOWN-n(u) "tú-ḫá

XXXVIII. "á-wa ī FORT-ĭ STONE? tú-mi-ḫa XXXIX. wa-tu-ta ă-śí-ī-da-wa-tà-ā-n(u)CITY "á-ti-ma-ī-n(a) tú-ḫa XL. kwa?-pa-wa-mu SEIZE-n(u) "^{d}WEATHER-GOD-ḫu-ī-ś. ^{d}DEER-HEAD-ī-ś.-ḫá "ś.-ta ī-da FORT-sa STONE tú-mi-n(u)

Phoenician

XIX. *w-bn 'nk hmjt 'zt b-kl qsjt 'l gblm b-mqmm* XX. *b-'š kn 'šm r'm b'l 'gddm* XXI. *'š bl 'š 'bd kn l-bt mpš* XXII. *w-'nk 'ztwd št-nm tht p'm-j*

XXXVIII. *w-bn 'nk h-qrt z* XXXIX. *w-št 'nk šm 'ztwdj* XL. *k b'l w-ršp ṣprm šlḫ-n l-bnt*

Phoenician:

Translation of the Phoenician Text:

"XIX. And I built strong forts at the frontiers on the spots XX. where there were evil men, gang-leaders, XXI. none of whom had been subject to the House of Mpš (dynasty of Asïtawadda), XXII. but I, Asïtawadda, laid them under my feet.

XXXVIII. And I built this city, XXXIX. and I gave (to it) the name Asïtawaddija (?), XL. for Baal (in hieroglyphic Hittite, "the Weather-god") and the Rešef of the birds (in hieroglyphic Hittite, "the Deer-god"?) sent me out to build (it)."

FIG. 48. Sentences XIX–XXII and XXXVIII–XL of the bilingual text of Karatepe. (Bossert, *Archiv Orientálni* XVIII, 3, pp. 24–25, and Bossert, *Jahrbuch für kleinasiatische Forschung* I, p. 272.)

meanings of words ascertained on the ground of the bilingual texts agree with those accepted prior to the knowledge of such texts. A part of the bilingual text of Karatepe is shown in Fig. 48. Thus, in the case of hieroglyphic Hittite, too, we have the unusual experience that the bilingual text is available not at the start of the research, but more or less at its close, as a welcome corroborating evidence. This is why it is incorrect to liken this bilingual find to the Rosetta Stone, as one occasionally hears it done.

In the preceding paragraph, I said advisedly that this bilingual text was found "more or less at the close" of the research, because the investigation of this not quite so simple script is still very far from its real conclusion. Namely, the inscriptions of Karatepe demonstrate absolutely clearly that the syllabic signs of the Hittite hieroglyphic writing show very many variants which still must be determined individually before the reading of the inscriptions can be called absolutely certain. And naturally only a minor portion of the many ideograms of this script appear in the Karatepe records corroborated as to meaning by the Phoenician translation. Also the vocabulary made certain by Karatepe is not all too large. It is important from the point of view of comparative linguistics that the Indo-European character of the language of the hieroglyphic texts and its close relationship to Luwian is more clearly recognizable now. Thus Karatepe is not only a welcome final confirmation of prewar research, but in many respects also a new beginning which warrants the hope that we may soon be nearer to a complete clarification of this problem, of equal interest to grammatologists and to linguists.

II. THE DECIPHERMENT AND STUDY OF OTHER SCRIPTS AND LANGUAGES OF THE OLD WORLD

THE research of the 19th and 20th centuries achieved its three great and, in a certain sense, classical feats of decipherment on the Egyptian writing, on the cuneiform script and on the Hittite hieroglyphics, and it derived from them the most valuable conclusions concerning the linguistic and cultural history of the ancient Orient. The decipherment of no other writing and the translation of no other language can quite match the value and significance of these three accomplishments. Yet, also those other decipherments and translations have many a feature or element worthy of universal attention and interest, and for this reason I shall outline here, more briefly, the most important ones.

In order to present a more comprehensive view, I shall classify the following reports in three groups, the first of which will comprise those instances where, analogously with the heretofore discussed three outstanding decipherments, the task involved both *the decipherment of an unknown writing and the interpretation of an unknown language*, the second will include the cases where only an *unknown writing* had to be deciphered, but the language written by it was a known one, and finally the third group will comprise the interpretations of *unknown languages* written in some known script (as in the case of cuneiform Hittite). But let it be stated right here and now that simple and clear-cut as the basis of the classification of a language into the first one of

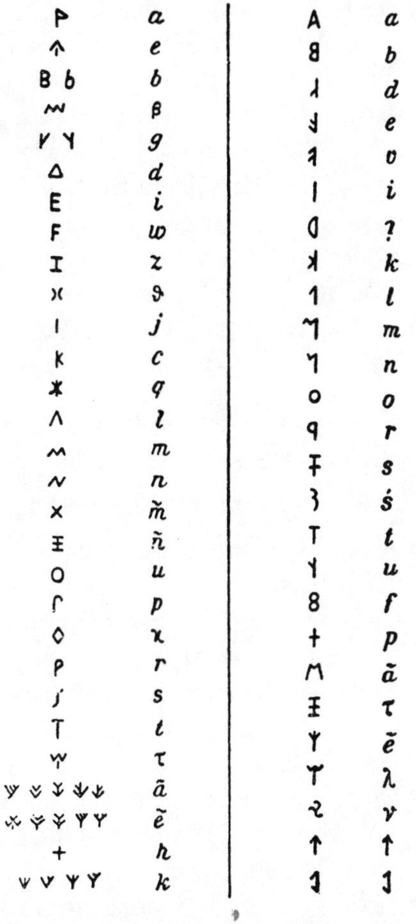

FIG. 49. The Lycian and Lydian alphabets. (From Friedrich, *Kleinasiatische Sprachdenkmäler*, p. 157.)

these three groups may seem to be, it is by no means so obvious and unambiguous. Namely, this particular group includes also Lycian and Lydian, two languages written in distinctly alphabetic scripts which are closely related to the

Greek alphabet (cf. Fig. 49), so that in these two instances we may speak of "decipherment" of scripts with qualifications only. Thus, the unlocking of the secrets of the inscriptions found in these two languages might be regarded also as purely linguistic interpretations, which would belong in our third group by definition. And the other two decipherments mentioned in our first group involve, objectively regarded, almost exclusively just a decipherment of the script where the translation of the language itself plays no part at all or a part of a mere secondary importance, so that these two cases might be assigned to our second group as well.

1. The Decipherment of Other Unknown Scripts and Languages

(a) *The Translation of the Lycian Language*

The language of Lycia, situated on the southwestern coast of Asia Minor, has been preserved in 150 inscriptions as well as in brief legends on coins, although the latter consist often of abbreviations and in general are of no help in the translation of the language. A few inscriptions have been known since the early part of the 19th century, but most of them were published only as a result of Austrian expeditions in 1884 and 1889. We are indebted to the Austrians also for the perfect publication by E. Kalinka of the Lycian inscriptions under the title *Tituli Lyciae lingua Lycia conscripti* (*Tituli Asiae Minoris*, Vol. I, Vienna, 1901). The bulk of the inscriptions are epitaphs, dating from the 5th and 4th centuries B.C., which differ from each other but little as to contents. Outstanding among the few inscriptions of other types is the lengthy text on the Xanthos Stela with its historical contents, although the language used in it is of such an ancient and so strongly dialectal form that our understanding of it is still very imperfect. Another fact to be considered is that determinatives, which are such excellent clues to the meanings of texts in cuneiform characters, are nonexistent in alphabetic scripts. The epitaphs are an easier problem because many of them are written bilingually in Lycian and Greek. The Greek text is, however, often a more or less free rendition of the meaning of the Lycian version.

I reproduce here two of these bilingual inscriptions, showing the Lycian texts in the customary Latin transliteration. Only inscription No. 117 of Kalinka's publication contains literally identical Greek and Lycian texts (Fig. 50):

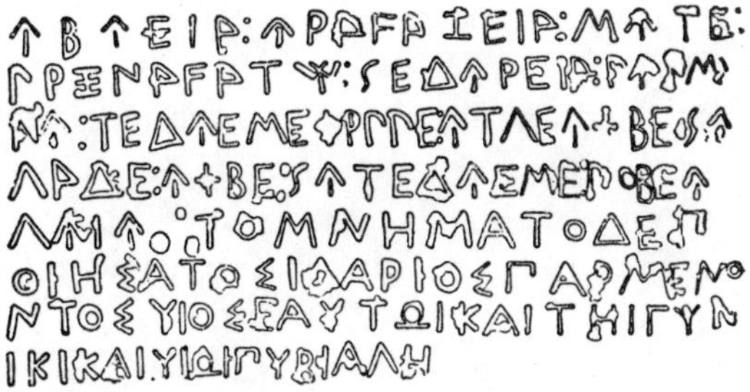

(1) *ebeija* : *erawazija* : *me ti* : (2) *prñnawatẽ* : *siderija* : *parm[ẽn]*- (3) *[ah]* : *tideimi [h]rppi* : *etli ehbi se* (4) *ladi* : *ehbi* : *se tideimi* : *pubie*- (5) *leje* : Τὸ μνῆμα τόδ' ἐπ- (6) οιήσατο Σιδάριος Παρμένο- (7) ντος υἱὸς ἑαυτῶι καὶ τῆι γυν[α]- (8) ικὶ καὶ υἱῶι Πυβιάληι.

FIG. 50. Lycian-Greek inscription No. 117. (From Kalinka, *Tituli Lyciae lingua Lycia conscripti.*)

The meaning of this inscription, according to the Greek text, is: "*This monument was made by Sidarios, the son of Parmenon, for himself and his wife and his son Pybiales.*" The word-for-word translation of the Lycian text is: "*This monument, now he who built (it), (is) Siderija, son of*

Parmena, for the own self and the own wife and the son Pubiele."

This yields the following translations of words: *ebe* = this; *erawazija* = monument (?); *prñnawatẽ* = he built; *tideimi* = son; *hrppi* = for; *etli* for *atli*, dative singular of *atla-* = self; *ehbi-* = own; *se* = and; *lada* = wife. The "*me ti*" introducing a sentence after a prefixed object contains the particle *me*, the meaning of which is more or less "now," and a pronoun, *ti*, which ought to be regarded as a relative one, meaning "who," rather than a demonstrative one, denoting "this," respectively "him, it." This *me ti* (*mẽ ti*) and the alternative expression *me ne* (*mẽ ne*) are not translated in the Greek text.

Let us consider now inscription No. 25a (Fig. 51):

Translation of the Greek text: "*Porpax,* (*son*) *of Thrypsis, nephew of Pyribates, the Tloan* i.e., a man from the city of Tlos, (*erected the statues*) *himself and his wife Tiseusembra, from Pinara, daughter of Ortakias, niece of Prianobas, for Apollo.*" Translation of the Lycian text: "*These statues* (?), *now /he who/ dedicated* (*them*) (*is*) *Kssbezẽ, son of Crupsse and nephew of Purihimete, the Tloan, the own self and the own wife Ticeucẽpre, the woman from Pille* = Pinara in Greek, *daughter of Urtaqija and niece of Prijenube.*"

This text adds only two word translations to those already known from the preceding inscription, viz.: *tuhes* = nephew or niece; *chatra* = daughter. The word *atru* (accusative singular) is a phonetic variant of *atlu* = the self. These two inscriptions will suffice to show that the word translations that can be gained from the bilingual texts are by no means too numerous. But the differences in the spelling of the names, chiefly in the second inscription, demonstrate furthermore that the Greeks were obviously not able accurately to represent the alien Lycian sounds and combinations of sounds with their

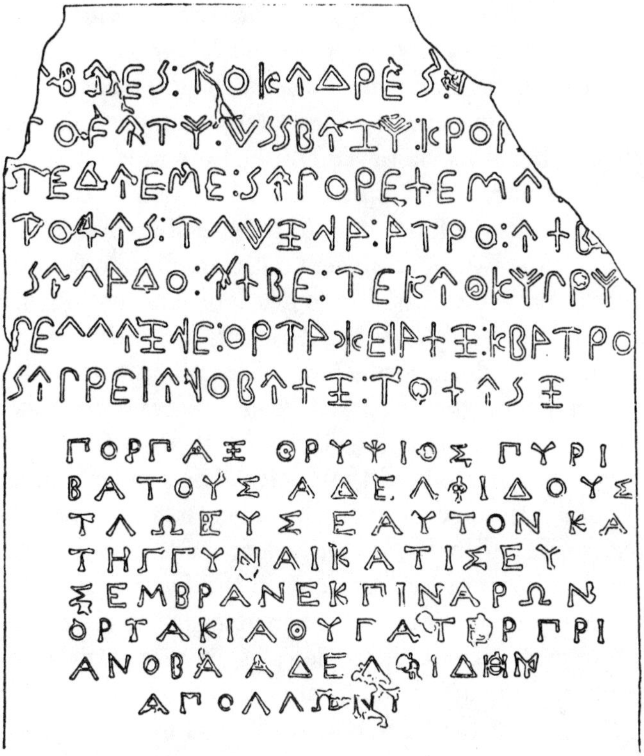

(1) *ebeis : tucedris : m[. . .]* (2) *tuwetẽ : kssbezẽ : crup[sseh]* (3) *tideimi : se purihime[teh]* (4) *tubes : tlãñna : atru : ebb[i]* (5) *se ladu : ebbi : ticeucẽprẽ* (6) *pilleñni : urtaqijahñ : cbatru* (7) *se prijenubehñ : tubesñ* (8) Πόρπαξ Θρύψιος Πυρι- (9) βάτους ἀδελ-φιδοῦς (10) Τλωεὺς ἑαυτὸν κα[ὶ] (11) τὴγ γυναῖκα Τισευ- (12) σέμβραν ἐκ Πινάρων (13) Ὀρτακία θυγατέρ⟨α⟩ Πρι- (14) ανόβα ἀδελφιδῆν (15) Ἀπόλλωνι.

FIG. 51. Lycian-Greek inscription No. 25a. (Kalinka, *Tituli Lyciae lingua Lycia conscripti.*)

own graphic resources (in one case, of course, the name in question is entirely different in the two languages—*Kssbezẽ* in Lycian, but *Porpax* in Greek). And the reader may well imagine that the research into the Lycian language encounters not only lexical and grammatical problems, but also a whole series of problems of a phonological character.

This branch of philological research is now over a hundred years old, but it has not accomplished too much in all that time. This poor record is attributable, insofar as the earlier period is concerned, not only to the use of an etymological method based without sufficient criticism on Indo-European linguistic principles, but also to a lack of sufficient linguistic material. It was only after the Austrians had discovered new inscriptions that the Frenchmen Six and Imbert and the Britisher Arkwright embarked on a perfect, systematic research in the 1880's. All three of them attempted to clarify the difficulties of the Lycian script and phonology. Six studied the Lycian coins in particular, which bore also Greek and Iranian names. Arkwright made a special study of the rendition of Greek names in the Lycian inscriptions and the representation of Lycian names in the Greek texts; the observed inaccuracies yielded all sorts of conclusions concerning spelling and pronunciation.

The study of Lycian obtained a second impetus from the work of the Scandinavian savants Bugge, Torp, Vilhelm Thomsen and Holger Pedersen, about the turn of the century. Laudatory mention is due above all to Thomsen's *Etudes lyciennes* (Copenhagen, 1899), a strongly combinatory analysis of the particles *me ne* (*mẽ ne*) and *me ti* (*mẽ ti*) which were used in Lycian to introduce sentences. The second standstill of the flourishing study of Lycian, soon after 1900, was caused by the lack of new, illustrative linguistic material, for not many new facts can be learned from the monotonous epitaphs.

Also the new departures made since 1928, after the progress in Hittitology, by Meriggi and by the old and yet still vigorously active Holger Pedersen, have not resulted in any permanent enlivenment. But they have at least definitely clarified the question of the linguistic affinities of Lycian. The opinions of linguists differed strongly even in the 20th century whether Lycian was to be considered a radically changed Indo-European language or some completely alien, possibly Caucasian tongue. In the course of the past two decades, the scales have tipped very strongly in favor of the Indo-European character of Lycian, and Pedersen set forth convincing arguments in his *Lykisch und Hittitisch** for a closer affinity of Lycian and the Indo-European languages of ancient Asia Minor, and specifically to Hittite, the best known of those languages.

(b) *The Translation of the Lydian Language*

Whereas more than a hundred years of study of Lycian have not netted more than a mere few painstakingly gained results, the study of Lydian has grown almost effortlessly out of nothing since World War I. A look into P. Kretschmer's *Einleitung in die Geschichte der griechischen Sprache*** will show what vague and insufficient notions people still had about this language in the last years of the 19th century. However, the scant number and monotonous nature of the linguistic records preclude very far-reaching results in this case, too.

The language of Lydia, situated on the western coast of Asia Minor, has been preserved in over 50 inscriptions, found chiefly in the course of American excavations at Sardes, the Lydian capital, in 1910–1913. Unfortunately, also in this

* "Lycian and Hittite."—*Det Kgl. Danske Videnskabernes Selskab, hist.-filol. Meddelelser* XXX 4, 1945.

** "Introduction to the History of the Greek Language."—Göttingen, 1896.—Cf. pp. 384–391.

case, most of the inscriptions are epitaphs dating from the 4th century B.C., and considerably similar in content, and only a few votive inscriptions and other texts deviate from the general pattern. The inscriptions were published in Vol. VI, Part II, of the encyclopedic work *Sardis* (Leiden, 1924).

A quick insight into the principles of this formerly completely unknown script and language was made possible by three bilingual texts. Two of these, two quite short *inscriptions in Lydian and Greek* (Fig. 52), though, would probably have been of very little help, but the third bilingual text, written in *Lydian and Aramaic* (Fig. 53), presented eight well legible lines in each version and thus promised a good

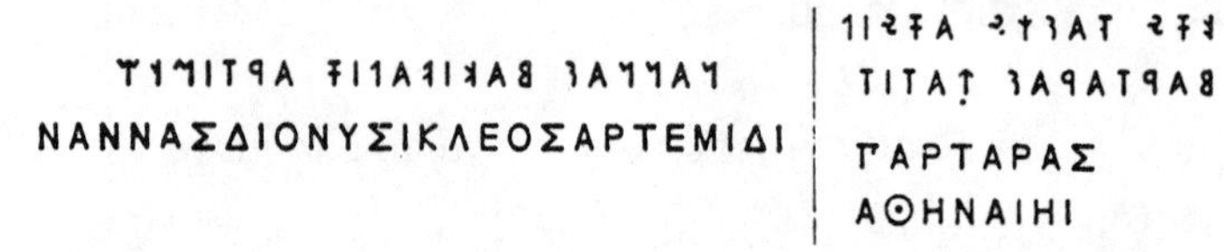

FIG. 52. The two Lydian-and-Greek bilingual texts. (From *Sardis*, Vol. VI: *Lydian Inscriptions*, Part II, Nos. 20 and 40.)

result. Aramaic, a Semitic language, was the language used by the various races of the Persian empire in their mutual dealings, and as such it was known in Lydia as well.

Let the two bilingual texts be quoted here word for word, for the sake of clarity (quoting the Lydian and Aramaic words transliterated in Latin characters). The first Lydian-and-Greek inscription (Sardis No. 20) reads:

nannaś bakivalis artimuλ Νάννας Διονυσικλέος ᾽Αρτέμιδι.

Translation: "Nannas, (*son*) *of Dionysikles* (*dedicates this statue*) *to Artemis*."

The name Nannas is identical in both languages; the Greek dative *Artemidi* is translated in Lydian by the oblique case

Artimuλ (nominative: *Artimuś*). The name of the father, *Dionysikles* in the Greek sentence, a derivate from the name of the god Dionysos, is rendered in Lydian as *Bakiva-*, certainly derived from the Lydian name of the same god, viz., Bakchos. Whereas the Greek uses the genitive case of the name, the Lydian text shows as adjective, *Bakiva-li*, meaning literally "the one of Bakiva."

FIG. 53. The bilingual text written in Lydian and Aramaic. (From Sardis, Vol. VI: *Lydian Inscriptions*, Part II, Plate I.)

Whereas the two short texts correspond to each other word for word, the Lydian version of the second inscription (Sardis No. 40) is more explicit than the Greek wording:

(1) *esv taśẽv asvil* (2) *bartaraś* ↑ *atit* (3) Παρτάρας (4) 'Αθηναίηι.

Translation of the Greek text: "*Partaras* (*dedicates this pillar*) *to Athene*."

In the Lydian portion, the Greek nominative *Partaras* is equalled by the Lydian form, of the same pronunciation, *Bartaraś*, and the Greek dative case *Athēnáēi* by the Lydian oblique case *Asvil* (*-l* = -λ in *Artimu*λ). It has been concluded by the combinatory method that *esv taśēv* (containing the demonstrative pronoun es-, "this," known from the third bilingual text) must mean "this pillar (?)"; ↑ *atit*, the phonetic value of the first character of which is uncertain, is presumably a verbal form, meaning, "erect(ed)" or "dedicate(d)" or something similar. Accordingly, the Lydian version means presumably, "*This pillar* (?) *dedicates* (or dedicated) *Bartaras to Athene*."

Far more information can be derived from the longer text written bilingually in Lydian and Aramaic, which reads, transliterated in Latin characters, as follows:

[LYDIAN]— [(1*) *borlλ* X *artakśassaλ paλmλuλ dãv*] (1) *[o]raλ islλ bakillλ est mrud eśśk [vãnaś]* (2) *laprisak pelak kudkit ist esλ vãn[aλ]* (3) *bλtarvod akad manelid kumlilid silukalid akit n[ãpis]* (4) *esλ mruλ buk esλ vãnaλ buk esvav* (5) *lapirisav bukit kud ist esλ vãnaλ bλtarvo[d]* (6) *aktin nãpis pelλk fēnsλifid fakmλ artimuś* (7) *ibśimsis artimuk kulumsis aaraλ biraλk* (8) *kλidaλ kofuλk piraλ pelλk bilλ v*↑ *bapēnt.*

/TRANSLATION/—/(1*) In the year 10 of Artaxerxes the king . . . in the/ (1) month (?)—on the fifth (??)—Bakillis. This stele and this /cavern/ and the wall (??) and the plot of land (?) and where (?) at this cavern (3) (there is) the antechamber, now this (is) belonging to Mane, the Kumli-son, the Siluka. Now who /soever/ (4) this stele or this cavern or this (5) wall (??) or where (?) at this cavern (is) the antechamber, (6) now who ever damages (?) whatsoever, now to him Artemis (7) the Ephesian and Artemis the Koloean courtyard and house, (8) earth and water, (real) property and whatsoever (is) his, shall scatter (?).

[ARAMAIC]— (1) *b* V *l-mrḥšwn̦ šnt* X *'rtḥšsš mlk'* (2) *b-sprd bjrt' znh stwn' w-m'rt' rdḥt'* (3) *'trt' w-prbr zj 'l sprb znh prbrb 'ḥr* (4) *zj mnj br kmlj srwkj* (?)' *w-'mn zj 'l stwn' znh 'w* (5) *m'rt' 'w l-rdḥt' l-qbl zj prbr l-m'rt'* (6) *znh 'ḥr mn zj jḥbl 'w jprk mnd'm 'ḥr* (7) *'rtmw zj klw w-'pššj trbṣh bjth* (8) *qnjnh ṭjn w-mjn w-mnd'mth jbdrwnh w-jpth.*

/TRANSLATION/—(1) On the fifth of (the month of) Markhešwān, year 10 of Artaxerxes the king, (2) in Sardes, the fortress. This stele and the cavern, the wall (??), (3) the plot of land (?) and the antechamber which at this sepulchral chamber (?) (is) the antechamber thereof, now (4) (this is) of Mane, the son of Kumli, the Siluka (?). And whosoever on this stele or (5) the cavern or on the wall (??), insofar as the antechamber at (6) this cavern (is), now whosoever destroys or mutilates whatsoever, now (7) Artemis of Koloe and of Ephesus shall his courtyard, his house, (8) his real property, earth and water, and whatsoever (is) his, to him scatter and to him break up."

The beginning of the Lydian version of this text is damaged, but it can be restored with certainty on the pattern of similar epitaphs. The Aramaic version contains a few words which are difficult problems even for Semitists, but it is clear on the whole nevertheless. Thus we obtain a reliable translation of the Lydian inscription, too, which in turn proves valuable in the translation of monolingual Lydian epitaphs, worded mostly along the same pattern. And, although this cannot be elucidated here in further particulars, we obtain a glimpse into a small section of the grammar and lexicon of the Lydian language, a glimpse which does give some notion of the language as a whole. Many scholars have tried to clarify the text written bilingually in Lydian and Aramaic, but particular laudatory mention is due to the thorough treatment given to it by Kahle, the Semitist, and Sommer, the Indo-European and Hittite specialist.

A certain difficulty was presented by the determination of the *phonetic values* of those Lydian characters which were not identical with the letters of the Greek alphabet. Even the names occurring in the bilingual inscription have not helped fully to establish the values of the still disputed characters, and there are a few rarely occurring symbols the phonetic values of which are still not known with any certainty. More disturbing still was the uncertainty about the frequently appearing symbols + and ϒ; the + was at first read as *h*, but now is read as *p*, whereas ϒ was at first regarded to mean ũ, but is now read as λ. The currently accepted reading of these characters is influenced by the Lydian word meaning "king," which appears in the inscriptions as ⊣ϒ𐤪ϒA+ (read from right to left) and has been recorded by Greek authors as *palmys.* We may therefore transliterate the Lydian word as *paλmλu-*, where λ, the Greek *lambda,* designates a variant of *l.* Thus, classical Greek literature is co-instrumental in this case in the deciphering of the Lydian alphabet.

The question of the *affinities* of the Lydian language has not been fully clarified as yet. Formerly, Herbig advocated the theory of a closer relationship with Etruscan, because according to Herodotus (I, 94), the Etruscans were supposed to have immigrated to Italy from Lydia. Nowadays, more credence is given to the opinion of Meriggi, that Lydian, like Lycian, is an Indo-European language, although strongly changed by alien linguistic influences. This view is based on similarities of the morphological systems, notably of the inflection of verbs, on similarities of certain pronouns, e.g., *amu* = *I* or *to me* (dative), *pis* = *who, pid* = *what* (cf.

Oscan *pis* and *pid*, Latin *quis* and *quid*), *nãpis* = *whosoever*, -*ad* = *it* (cf. Hittite -*at* = *it*), *kud* = *where*, as well as on certain individual words, such as *bira*- = *house*, the Hittite equivalent of which is *pir*—not to mention uncertain etymologies. In this case, too, the paucity of linguistic material prevents the formation of a comprehensive view.

(c) *On the Translation of the Language of Side*

We are told by the Greek historian Arrian (cf. *Anabasis I*, 26:4) that the city of Side, in Pamphylia, on the southern coast of Asia Minor, had a language of its own in the days of classical Greece. Specimens of this language, in an undecipherable script, were known even in the 19th century A.D.; they were inscriptions on coins dating from the 4th and 5th centuries B.C., but they were so brief that they defied the most concentrated efforts of Waddington (1861), Friedländer (1877 and 1883) and Six (1897) who were unable to decipher them.

A short inscription in Greek and Sidetic was found by the Italian excavators Paribeni and Romanelli in Side in 1914 (Fig. 54). But also that text was too short to enable the investigators to decipher it, especially since also the Greek portion of it was not legible clearly and unambiguously. Only

FIG. 54. The Artemon inscription, written in Greek and Sidetic. (From Bossert, *Belleten* 14, Fig. 2.)

in 1949, in the course of new excavations in Side, did Bosch find another, somewhat longer and well legible inscription, written bilingually in Sidetic and Greek, which enabled Bossert to make a certain headway in the decipherment of the Sidetic script. (See Fig. 55.)

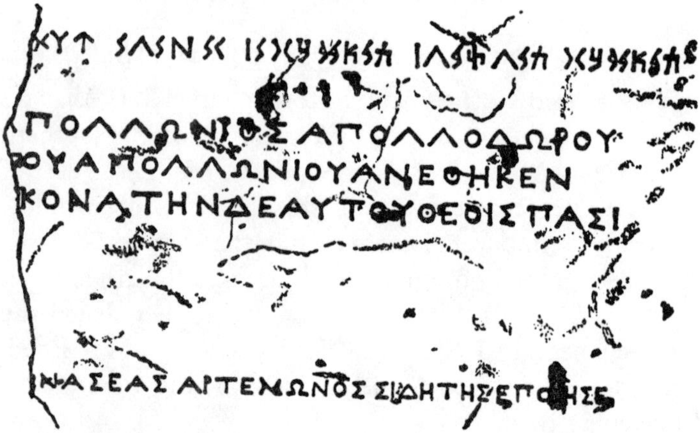

FIG. 55. The Apollonios inscription, written bilingually in Sidetic and Greek. (From Bossert, *Belleten 14*, Fig. 4.)

I quote here first the Greek text of the second bilingual inscription:

(1) [᾿Α]πολλώνιος ᾿Απολλοδώρου (2) [τ]οῦ ᾿Απολλωνίου ἀνέθηκεν (3) [εἰ]κόνα τήνδ᾿ ἑαυτοῦ θεοῖς πᾶσι.

The translation of this Greek sentence is: "*Apollonios,* (*son*) *of Apollodoros,* (*the son*) *of Apollonios, erected this image of himself for all gods.*"

In this instance, both the dedicator and his grandfather are called Apollonios, and also the name of the father, Apollodoros, is derived from the name of the god Apollo. These consistencies must recur in the Sidetic portion. And the first and third words of that text do actually appear to have the same identical stem, even though their flexional (declensional) endings differ, and at least the initial portion of the second word is similar. On the ground of this observation, Bossert transliterated the Sidetic text tentatively as follows: *p-u-l-u-n-i?-o?? p-u-r-d-u-r-s?? p-u-l-u-n-i?-o??-a-s??* m-a-ś?-a-r-a?-e?-o??-[. . . . .].

The results thus obtained encouraged him to re-examine the older bilingual text once again, and he decided that it had to be read as follows:

Ἀθηνᾶ[. . . . .] Ἀρ:έμων Ἀθηνίππου (?) χαριστήρια *?-i?-a θ-a-n-d? a-r-t-m-u-n θ-a-n-p-i?-o??-s?? m-a-?-s??-o??-a-?-a-s??*

The translation of the Greek part is: "*Athena* . . . . . *Artemon*, (*son*) *of Athenippos*, (*dedicates*) *thank-offering.*"

The determination of the phonetic values of a number of characters represents the entire progress that we have been able to accomplish in the domain of the Sidetic inscriptions to this date. New results, above all with respect to the linguistic forms and linguistic affinities, may be expected only after the discovery of new inscriptions.

(d) *The Decipherment of the Numidian Script*

Another script and language, the translation of which is deserving of being mentioned here, are the products of quite another part of the Old World; they are the script and language of ancient Numidia, which once occupied what is today Algeria and Tunisia, in North Africa.

The Numidians, members of the Berber race, were at first economically, culturally, and also politically dependent on Carthage; during the second Punic war (218–201 B.C.), with Roman backing, they became an independent, unified nation under Masinissa, and in the 2nd century B.C. they built a mighty empire in North Africa which expanded at the expense of the constantly more and more subdued Carthaginian state, until it became a tributary of Rome.

The political and cultural independence of the Numidians manifested itself also in the creation of an alphabetic, or rather purely consonantal, script which has been preserved to our days in more than a thousand inscriptions, most of them brief and often casually written epitaphs. Thugga, the modern Dougga in Tunisia, is the only place where also a few official building inscriptions in the Numidian language have been preserved. A variant of this script is still being used today by the desert tribes of the Tuareg, although with such individually and independently developed forms that the modern script cannot be used for the decipherment of the ancient writing.

Fortunately, though, there are quite a few bilingual inscriptions available and helpful in the decipherment of the Numidian alphabet (Fig. 56). The Numidians wrote their inscriptions not only in their own language but frequently in Punic or Latin as well, and by this date nine epitaphs written bilingually in Punic and Numidian and about fifteen in Latin and Numidian are known. Their value must, however, not be overestimated because it is a peculiarity of both the monolingual and multilingual Numidian inscriptions that they are limited to the naming of names and are not concerned about stating other facts. Building inscriptions list conscientiously the names of all craftsmen who had anything at all to do with the construction. These many names appearing in the bilingual Numidian inscriptions are a welcome aid to help us determine the phonetic values of the characters of the Numidian alphabet with absolute clarity at least.

As an example of bilingual texts written in Numidian and Punic, I reproduce here the big inscription discovered on a

•	•	ʾ(alpha)	‖	=	l
⊙	⊙ ▫	b	⊐⊃	⊔∪	m
⌐←	∨∧	ǧ	ǀ	ǀ	n
⊓	⊐⊏	d	X	X 8	s
‖‖	‖‖	h	⊏⟨⦿	⊓	s²
=	‖	w	≡ ÷	‖‖ •ǀ•	ǧ (y)
−	—	z	X	XX δ	p (f)
H	H I	ẓ		≡	q
⋀	⊔	z̄			
⊢	⊥⊤	ḥ	O	O ⊐	r
⟩⊢	⊓	ṭ, ḍ	⩾	M⩽	š
Z	N Z	ỉ	+ X	+	t
⇐	⇑	k	⊐	⊔	t²

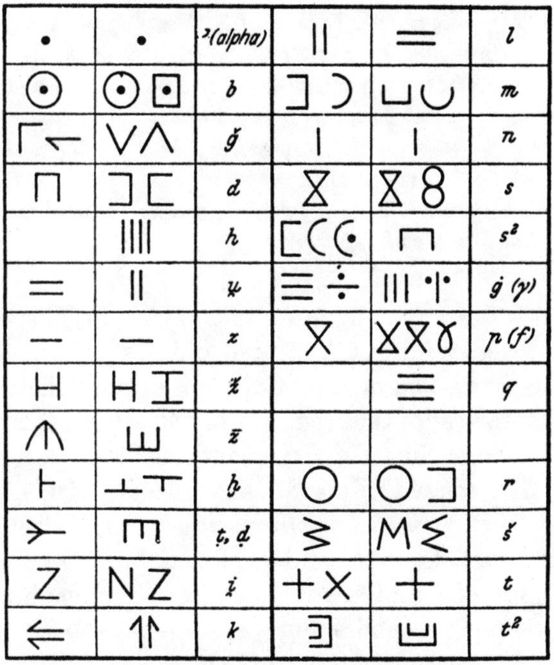

FIG. 56. The Numidian alphabet. (From Jensen,
Die Schrift, Fig. 102.)

temple of Masinissa in 1904 (Fig. 57). I indicate here also
the transliteration of both texts, in Latin characters, as well
as a translation, as follows:

[PUNIC]—(1) *t mqdš z bnʾ bʿlʾ Tbgg l-Msnsn h-mmlkt bn Gʿjj
h-mmlkt bn Zllsn h-šft b-št ʿsr š-[mlk]* (2) *Mkwsn b-št Šft h-mmlkt bn
ʾfšn h-mmlkt rbt mʾt Šnk bn Bnj w-Šft bn Ngm bn Tnkw* (3) *mṣṣkwj
Mgn bn Jrštn bn Sdjln w-gzbj Mgn bn Šft rb mʾt bn ʿbdʾšmn h-m[ml]kt*
(4) *gldgjml Zmr bn Msnf bn ʿbdʾšmn h-ʾd[r] ḥmšm h-ʾš Mqlʾ bn ʾšjn
h-mmlkt bn Mgn h-mml[kt]* (5) *tnʾm ʿl h-mlkt z ʾšjn bn ʾnkkn bn
Ptš w-ʾrš bn Šft bn Šnk*

[NUMIDIAN]—(6) *ṣk[n] . Tbgg . bnjfš? . Msnsn . gldṯ . w-Gjj . gldṯ . w-Zllsn . šfṭ* (7) *sbsndb . gldṯ . sjsb . gld . Mkwsn* (8) *Šfṭ . gldṯ . w-Fšn . gldṯ . mwsnḥ . Šnk . w-Bnj . w-Šnk . d-Šfṭ . w-M[gn?]* (9) *w-Tnkw . mṣṣkw . Mgn . w-Jrštn . w-Sdjln . gẓb . Mgn . w-Šfṭ . mw[snb]* (10) *w-Šmn . gldṯ . gldgmjl . Zmr . w-Msnf . w-Šmn . gldmṣk . M[ql'?]* (11) *w-Šjn . gldṯ . w-Mgn . gldṯ . ṭnjn . Šjn . w-Nkkn . w-Pṭš . d-R[š]* (12) *<w->Šfṭ . w-Šnk* (PUNIC) *w-b-bn'm Hn' bn Jtnb'l bn Ḥnb'l w-Nfṭsn bn Šfṭ*

/TRANSLATION OF THE PUNIC VERSION/—(1) This temple /accusative case/ there built the citizens of Thugga for King Masinissa, son of King Gaja, son of the Suffete Zllsn, in the tenth year of the reign (2) of Micipsa, in the year of King Šfṭ, son of King 'fšn. Commanders of the one hundred /were/ Šnk, son of Bnj, and Šfṭ, son of Ngm /Magon?/, son of Tnkw. (3) Mṣṣkwj /*an official title*/ /was/ Magon, son of Jrštn, son of Sdjln. And gzbj /*another title*/ /was/ Magon, son of Šfṭ, of the commander of the one hundred, of the son of King 'Abdešmun. (4) Gldgjml /*another title*/ /was/ Zmr, son of Msnf, son of 'Abdešmun. Leader (?) of the fifty men /was/ Mql', son of King 'šjn, son of King Magon. (5) In charge of this work /were/ 'šjn, son of 'nkkn, son of Pṭš, and Ariš, son of Šfṭ, son of Šnk. ..... (12) And the architects /were/ Hanno, son of Jatanbaal, son of Hannibal, and Nfṭsn, son of Šfṭ.

Fig. 58 shows two epitaphs as examples of the scantier Latin- and Numidian inscriptions. These two specimens show at the same time also the customary direction of the Numidian script which ran *from the bottom to the top* (the only exceptions being the inscriptions of Thugga in which this convention yielded to the Punic custom of writing from right to left). As it can be seen, the Latin versions of both inscriptions indicate also the ages of the deceased, 75 years in the first and 70 years in the second one, whereas these

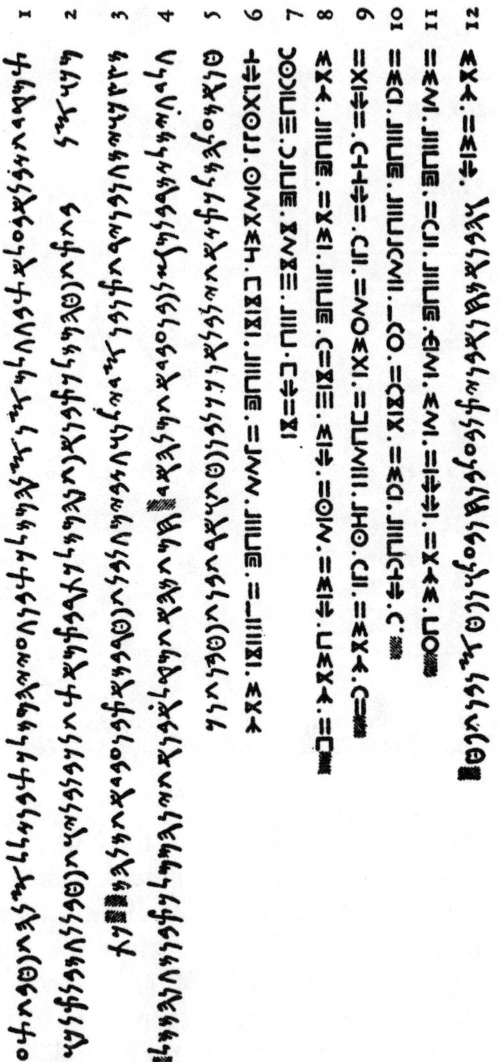

FIG. 57. The Masinissa Inscription, written bilingually in Punic and Numidian. (From Chabot, *Recueil des inscriptions Libyques*, No. 2.)

numbers seem to be missing from the Numidian portions. The words *msw* and *mnkd* are Numidian titles.

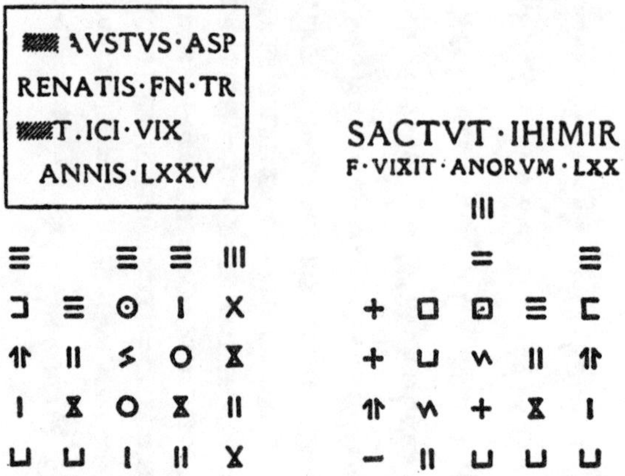

a) = CIL VIII 17317.

h		h	h	h	
d	h	b	n	t	
k	w	j	r	s	
n	s	[b]	s	w	↑
m	m	n	w	f	

b) = CIL VIII 5220 and 17395.

			h		
			l		h
	t	r	b	h	d
	t	m	j	w	k
↑	k	j	t	s	n
	z	w	m	m	m

Fig. 58. Two bilingual (Latin and Numidian) inscriptions. (From Chabot, *Recueil des inscriptions Libyques*, Nos. 85 and 151.)

It is comparatively easy to decipher the Numidian script on the strength of the bilingual inscriptions. Although these inscriptions, because of the very nature of the texts, give but quite incomplete information concerning the Numidian language, they justify certain conclusions in that respect as well. Thus, the Masinissa inscription permits us to recognize *gld* (as well as its derivative, *gldṭ*) as the Numidian word for "king." In every inscription, wherever the father of somebody is named, there occurs the short word *-w*, for "son"; a heavily damaged inscription, written bilingually in Numidian and Punic, not illustrated in this book, makes evident the meaning of two designations of occupations, viz.: *nbb-n n šqr'* means "wood-cutters," and *nbṭ-n n zl'* means "iron-founders" (both plural). Rössler recognized the verbal form *eṣkan* ("they built") in the first word of the Masinissa inscription, written as *ṣk*[*n*]. Even this meager linguistic material makes it evident that, insofar as the vowelless consonantal skeleton of the language justifies a conclusion, the Numidian language of antiquity is identical with the Berber spoken, as a secondary language to Arabic, in North Africa today, or in other words, that the Berber language has practically not changed at all in the course of two thousand years. This is a valuable conclusion, reached despite the scantiness of the linguistic material available.

2. The Decipherment of Other Unknown Scripts

The actual translation of a language played a part of minor importance even in the decipherment of the Sidetic and Numidian records, but the two cases which we shall discuss next go even further and can truly be regarded as cases of pure decipherment, because it could be presupposed in each case that the language of the inscriptions was a known one.

There is a case which I even omit altogether, although it would belong in this chapter, namely the decipherment by Vilhelm Thomsen of the *Early Turkish* (*Türki*) *runic writing* (appearing in inscriptions dating from the 8th century A.D., found in various parts of Siberia and Mongolia) because this script is not of the ancient Near East and thus lies both temporally and spatially beyond the range of the present book, and also because its decipherment offers hardly anything new technically. It resembles the decipherment of the Ugaritic writing (p. 84 *et seq.*), in that the decipherer assumed beforehand that the inscriptions were in a certain specific language, and he determined the phonetic values of the unknown characters, without any bilingual text to help him, but assisted by the knowledge of the structure of the language, the way a cryptographer decodes a modern, artificial secret writing.

(a) The Decipherment of the Cypriote Script

The Greeks of Cyprus, whose ancestors had settled on the island about the turn of the 2nd millennium B.C. to the first, did not use the same script as all the other Greeks in later historic times, but employed a peculiar syllabic writing, written from right to left, which knows syllables only of the consonant + vowel type and is very poorly suited to the

Vowels	a	e	i	o	u
j	ja	je	—	—	—
v	va	ve	vi	vo	—
r	ra	re	ri	ro	ru
l	la	le	li	lo	lu
m	ma	me	mi	mo	mu
n	na	ne	ni	no	nu
Labials	pa	pe	pi	po	pu
Dentals	ta	te	ti	to	tu
Gutturals	ka	ke	ki	ko	ku
s	sa	se	si	so	su
z	za	—	—	zo	—
x	xa	xe	—	—	—

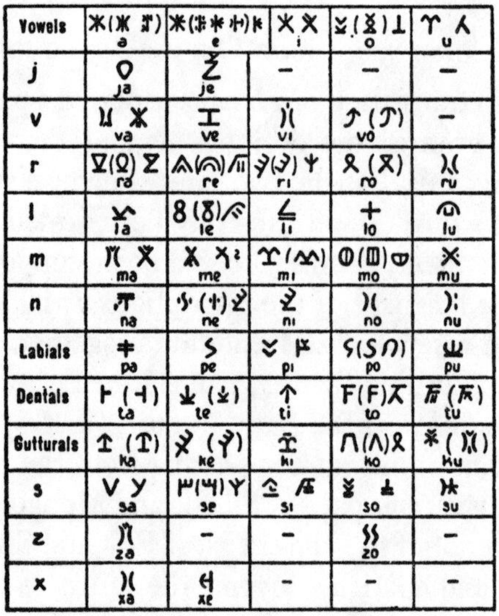

FIG. 59. The Cypriote syllabary. (From Thumb, *Handbuch der griechischen Dialekte*, p. VII.)

Greek language. In other words, the Greeks of Cyprus had left the mother country on the continent before the introduction of the alphabetic writing and adopted in Cyprus the principles of writing of an entirely different race.

Since Greek looks very strange when written with the characters of the Cypriote syllabary (Fig. 59), a few comments are indicated concerning the writing conventions of the Greeks of Cyprus. In writing syllables containing plosives, the user of this syllabary cannot distinguish lemis, fortis and aspirates, i.e., *d*, *t* and θ, or *b*, *p* and *ph*, or *g*, *k* and χ, but can write only *t*, *p* and *k*, in other words *ta* for *da*, *ta* and θ*a*, *pi* for *bi*, *pi* and *phi*, *etc*. This script does not distinguish, as does the Greek writing in the cases of *e* and *o*, between long and short vowels, so that, e.g., *o-ne-te-ke* is written for ὀνέθηκε (*onéthēke*) = "he erected" (Attic: ἀνέθηκε). Nasals are not indicated when preceding a consonant, e.g.: *pa-ta* for πάντα (*pánta*) = "everything." Consonants occurring at the end of a syllable are written with an unpronounced auxiliary vowel, mostly e: *ka-re* for γάρ (gar) = "for, thus"; *te-o-i-se* for θεοῖς (*theoīs*) = "to the gods"; *to-ko-ro-ne* for τὸ(ν) χῶρον (*to/n/ chōron*) = "the room" (*accusative*). The occurrence of two or more adjacent consonants at the beginning or in the middle of a syllable is likewise prevented by the interpolation of an unpronounced vowel between the consonants; when the group of consonants would occur in the initial position, the first syllable symbol contains the same vowel as the second one, e. g., *Sa-ta-si-ka-ra-te-se* for Στασικράτης (*Stasikrátēs*, a name), but in a medial position the vowel contents of the two syllable symbols are identical only if the group can occur in an initial position, too, e.g., *A'po-ro-ti-ta-i* for 'Αφροδίται (*Aphrodítāi*) = "of Aphrodite," but otherwise the interpolated vowel will be identical with the vowel immediately preceding the consonant group, e.g., *a-ra-ku-ro* for ἀργύρω (argýrō) = "of the silver." Since Cypriote Greek shows many a deviation from standard Greek linguistically, too, it is easily understandable that in many instances no certain reading can be established at all. Thus, a word written as *a-to-ro-po-se* can be read as ἄνθρωπος (*ánthrōpos*) = "man," but also as ἄτροπος (*átropos*) = "immutable," as ἄτροφος (átrophos) = "not (well) fed," and finally also as ἄδορπος (*ádorpos*) = "not dined."

Inscriptions, coins and medals from Cyprus bearing this script began to be known about 1850. It could not be suspected at first that they were written in the Greek language but in an alien script. The scholars of those days did not yet know the several bilingual records, in Cypriote and Phoenician as well as in Cypriote and standard Greek, which we know today, so that the new domain of research remained a playground of fantastic hypotheses until 1870 or so.

R. H. Lang, a Britisher, published the first *Phoenician-and-Cypriote bilingual inscription* in 1872; that was the inscription which was published by the Semitists in the *Corpus Inscriptionum Semiticarum I* 89, and by the Hellenists in Collitz-Bechtel's *Sammlung der griechischen Dialekt-Inschriften* (Göttingen, 1883–1915) as No. 59 (Schwyzer, *Dialectorum Graecarum exempla epigraphica potiora*, Leipzig, 1923, No. 680), and which is reproduced in this book as Fig. 60. It is a votive inscription addressed by a Phoenician nobleman by the name of Baalrōm to Apollo of Amyklai in the fourth year of the reign of the Phoenician king Milkjaton of Idalion and Kition, i.e., in 388 B.C. The Phoenician portion is strongly damaged, but it can be completed easily according to similarly worded inscriptions originating from the time of the same monarch. The names in the inscription thus furnished the fundamental clues for the decipherment, and the use of a point for separation mark between words facilitated the task. Since the word "king" occurred in the inscription twice, Lang already suspected that a certain group of symbols represented the name and title of King Milkjaton.

George Smith ingeniously carried the decipherment a long step forward almost at the same time. He, too, concentrated at first on the names *Milkjaton, Idalion* and *Kition*. The great number of characters (about 55) suggested to Smith from the very start that the Cypriote script was not alphabetic but syllabic. This opinion was corroborated in his mind by the fact that the geographic names *Idalion* and *Kition* did not end, as could be expected in view of the Greek form, in the same vowel, *-i*; thus, the *-i* in the ending of both geographic names had to be contained already in the syllabic symbol (the Cypriote forms are, reading from right to left, ↑ʑ = *Ke-ti-*, and ≤⊢✱ = *E-da-li-*). On the other hand, he encountered the *l* of *Milkjaton* (more precisely, that is, the syllabic sign ≤ /*li*/ of *Mi-li-ki-ja-to-ne*) in the word *Idalion.*

Also Smith recognized the word which Lang had already assumed to mean "king." It occurs in two places, with a different ending in each, but Smith reasoned that the reason was that it was used in two different declensional cases, first in the genitive and then—as Smith assumed, erroneously—in the nominative. The question as to what language other than the Cypriote changed the *penultimate* phoneme of the word meaning "king" in the course of its declension, led Smith to the *Greek* word for "king," *basileús* (genitive singular: *basiléōs*) and he concluded—rather superficially, and yet, as we know today, correctly—that the Cypriote inscriptions were written in the Greek language. This conclusion decided the direction of the further work of decipherment.

With the aid of the names and of the word *basileus*, Smith determined the phonetic values of eighteen syllable signs with a certain degree of probability. With their aid he tried then to make headway in reading the brief inscriptions on

(I) PHOENICIAN:

(1) *[b-jmm x l-jrḥ y] b-šnt 'rb' 4 l-mlk . Mlkjtn [mlk]*
(2) *[Ktj w-'djl sml] 'z 'š jtn w-jtn' . 'dnn . B'lr[m]*
(3) *[bn 'bdmlk l-'l]-j l-Ršp Mkl . k šm' ql-j brk*

"(1) /On the xth day of the month of y/ in the year 4 of King Milkjaton, /king/
"(2) /of Kition and Idalion./ This (is) /the image/ which gave and erected our Lord B'alrōm,
"(3) /the son of 'Abdimilk, for/ his /god/ Rešef of Mkl, for he listened to his voice. He bless(ed?) (him.)"

(II) CYPRIOTE GREEK:

(a) In the syllabic script of the original:

(1) *[i to-i | te?-ta?-ra?-to?-i? | ve-te-i] | pa-si-le-vo-se | mi-li-ki-ja-to-no-se | ke-ti-o-ne | ka-te?-ta-li-o-ne | pa-si-le-u-*
(2) *[-o?-to?-se? | ta-ne e-pa-ko]-me-na-ne | to pe-pa-me-ro-ne | ne-vo-so-ta-ta-se | to-na-ti-ri-ja-ta-ne | to-te ka-te-se-ta-se | o va-na-xe |*
(3) *[Pa?-a?-la?-ro?-mo?-se? |] o A-pi-ti-mi-li-ko-ne | to A-po-lo-ni | to A-mu-ko?-lo-i | a-po-i vo-i | ta-se e-u-ku-la?-se*
(4) *[e]-pe-tu-ke i tu-ka-i | a-za?-ta-i |*

(b) Modern Greek transliteration:

(1) [ἰ(ν) τῶ̄ι | τετάρτω̄ι? | Ϝέτει] | βασιλῆ̄Ϝος | Μιλκιjάθω̄νος |
Κε̄τίω̄ν | κατ (?) Ἐδαλίω̄ν | βασιλεύ-
(2) [ο(ν)τος? | τᾶν ἐπαγο]μενᾶν τῶ̄ πε(μ)παμέρω̄ν | νεϜοστάτας |
τὸν | ἀ(ν)δριjά(ν)ταν | τό(ν)δε κατέστασε | ὁ Ϝάναξ |
(3) [Βααλρω̄μος? |] ὁ Ἀβδιμίλκω̄ν | τῶ̄ι Ἀπόλ(λ)ω̄νι | Ἀμυκλω̄ι |
ἀφ' ὦ̄ι Ϝοι | τᾶς εὐχω̄λᾶς
(4) [ἐ]πέτυχε· ἰ(ν) τύχαι | ἀζαθᾶι.

"(1) /In the fourth year when/ King Milkjaton over Kition and Edalion rule—
"(2) /-d/, on the last day of the five-day period of the /intercalary/ days, did this statue erect the Prince
"(3) /Ba'alrōm,/ the (son?) of 'Abdimilk, for Apollo of Amyklai, after he for himself the desire
"(4) had accomplished; in good luck!"

FIG. 60. Phoenician-and-Cypriote bilingual inscription of Idalion. (From R. H. Lang, *Transactions of the Society of Biblical Archaeology I*, 1872, Table following p. 128.)

the medals which presumably contained nothing but names —Greek names, as Smith now assumed. He identified in them, for instance, the male names *Euagoras, Euelthon, Stasioikos, Pythagoras* (rather *Philokypros!*), *Stasiagoras* (rather *Stasikypros!*) etc.

The failure of Smith to continue his decipherment, which he had begun quite correctly on the whole, must be attributable to his scant knowledge of the Greek language. Thus Birch, the Egyptologist, published the much-needed explicit proof to the effect that the Cypriote language, according to the evidence of its linguistic structure, could not be any Semitic or Egyptian tongue, but only a variant of Greek. The Greek of the inscriptions, as Birch read them, seemed still to be remarkably barbaric and corrupt. This impression was due partly to the incorrect way in which several syllabic signs were still being read—a syllabic writing represents always a more difficult problem for the decipherer than an alphabetic script, just because of the greater number of individual signs in a syllabary—and partly also to the ignorance of the decipherers as regards the peculiarities, now being gradually clarified, of the quite odd Cypriote Greek dialect.

Johannes Brandis, the German numismatist who regrettably died at such an early age, identified the word meaning "and," and by this important discovery he made a better analysis also of the monolingual inscriptions possible. According to the Greek lexicographer Hesychos, the Cypriote word for "and" was *kas*, instead of the *kai* of standard Greek, and Brandis found this *kas* in the inscriptions. He determined also the phonetic values of further syllabic signs. Since the Greek character of the language was already an established fact, the decipherers were no longer restricted to using solely the few and scant bilingual inscriptions in their work, and they were free to determine the phonetic values of the still questionable syllabic signs from the tolerably intelligible sentences and phrases found in monolingual inscriptions, on the basis of their knowledge of the Greek language.

The long monolingual bronze inscription of Idalion, published by Moriz Schmidt, a Hellenist of Jena, in 1874, proved to be particularly important. Schmidt succeeded with the aid of this text in establishing the phonetic values of a great number of further syllabic signs, by the combinatory method, and also in definitely determining the basic features and principles of the Cypriote writing, viz., that it consists solely of syllabic signs which may represent a single vowel or a consonant followed by a vowel, but no other combination.

Deecke and Siegismund brought the decipherment essentially to its conclusion. Their important accomplishment consisted in the elimination of the last difficulties in the reading of the Cypriote script, by establishing the phonetic values of syllabic signs denoting syllables beginning with the phonemes /j/ or /w/. The subsequent linguistic study of details need not concern us here any further.

The somewhat perfunctory conclusion of George Smith that the Cypriote inscriptions were written in Greek proved to be no less correct than the likewise hasty conclusion of Hans Bauer concerning the West Semitic character of the Ugaritic language. Moreover, also those scholars are being proven right who claimed that this script, so unsuited to the Greek language, had been borrowed from another race. A few inscriptions from Cyprus which have been known since 1910, are written in the same Cypriote script, but in a non-Greek language which is being regarded, with full justification, as the still unknown language of the non-Indo-European autochthonous population of Cyprus. We know even an inscription written bilingually in that unknown language and in the Attic Greek of the 4th century B.C. This inscription still appears to be untranslatable, despite an attempt by Bork, because of the shortness of the Greek portion in particular. But the names of persons can be identified, even though showing certain discrepancies, in the two versions, and they prove that the phonetic values of the syllabic symbols are the same in the alien language as in the Cypriote-Greek inscriptions.

(b) *On the Decipherment of the Proto-Byblic Script*

I still have to discuss here the decipherment of the ancient inscriptions from Byblos, a city on the northern Phoenician coast. They are written in a peculiar script, partly resembling pictograms and partly cursive in shape; the French Dhorme, one of the scholars who deciphered the Ugaritic writing (cf. p. 84) attempted its decipherment in 1946, but his efforts have still not produced any clear and definite results.

Byblos was one of the oldest cultural centers of Phoenicia; its close relationship with Egypt originated as far back as the beginning of the 3rd millennium B.C. and was still maintained in the 2nd millennium B.C. The oldest known inscriptions of Byblos written in the Phoenician alphabetic script date from about 1000 B.C., but written records had been made in that city, obviously, prior to that date, too. Egyptian inscriptions appear on sarcophagi from the early 2nd mil-

FIG. 61. Stone inscription in the Proto-Byblic script. (From Dunand, *Byblia Grammata*, Fig. 26.)

lennium; according to the evidence found in the archives of El-Amarna, Egypt (cf. p. 3), Byblos used the Babylonian cuneiform script and the Akkadian language for international communications. In addition to these alien, and perhaps just occasionally used, systems of writing, the special script to be discussed here can be observed on two well preserved bronze tablets, a damaged stone tablet and three fragments of stone tablets, as well as four bronze spatulae, all of which are to be regarded on archaeological grounds as dating from the early part of the 2nd, if not the late part of the 3rd millennium B.C., and which for that very reason I would like to name *Proto-Byblic*, i.e., Early Byblos script. All the inscriptions were published by M. Dunand in his book, *Byblia Grammata* (Beyrouth, 1945), on pages 71–135. (Cf. Figs. 61 and 62.)

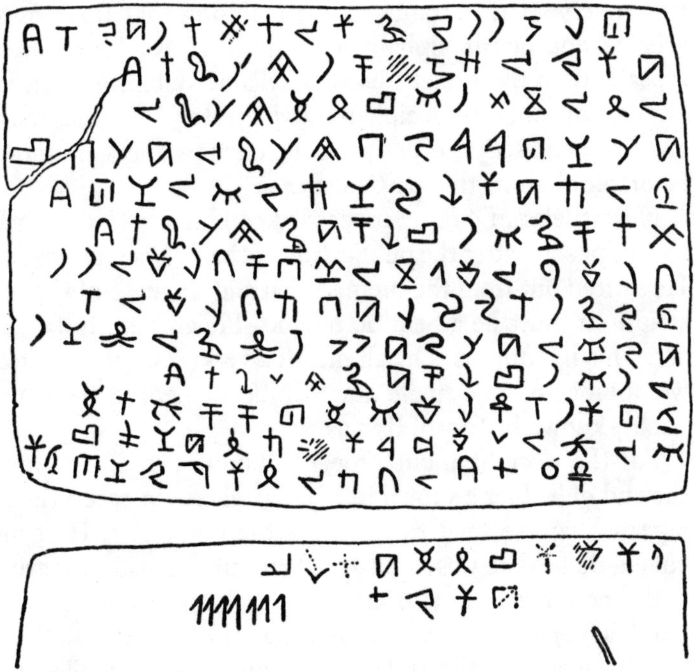

FIG. 62. Proto-Byblic bronze tablet c. (From Dunand, *Byblia Grammata*, Fig. 28.)

The prospects of a successful decipherment are not very favorable, for the following reasons: There exist *no bilingual texts* or similar references. The *number of the texts is not high*. Only one of the two undamaged bronze tablets runs as long as 41 lines, the other one is only 15 lines long, the spatulae bear very short texts, and even the biggest one of the damaged stone tablets bears only 10 lines of writing. Only on one of the four spatulae are the words separated by vertical strokes, in the other inscriptions *the words are not separated.* Moreover, the *number of symbols* is quite *high;* 114 different symbols have been distinguished to this date. This circumstance very soon warranted the conclusion that this was a *syllabic,* and not an alphabetic, script. And as I have stated repeatedly in the present book, a syllabic system of writing always confronts the decipherer with greater difficulties than an alphabetic script, even when the circumstances are more favorable than in this particular case.

Nevertheless, Dhorme proceeded confidently to decipher the script soon after the publication of the *Byblia Grammata.* He started out from the premise that the language of the inscriptions must be a Semitic tongue—Phoenician, to be exact. This hypothesis is by all means a very plausible one, for we cannot find one single non-Semitic element in the thoroughly known history of Byblos.

For the decipherment proper, Dhorme proceeded from the end of Tablet c shown in Fig. 62, where the seven times repeated sign seemed to represent the numeral 7. He concluded that a date was indicated there, and he read the entire 15th line tentatively as *b-šnt* 7, "in the year 7," "in the 7th year." The reason for which Dhorme transliterates vowelless Semitic words in the style of the later Semitic alphabetic writing, is not that he considers the Proto-Byblic script a consonantal system of writing. In view of the high number of characters, he is convinced that this is a syllabic writing, with specific signs for the syllables *ba, bi, bu, ša, ši, šu* (possibly also for *ab, ib, ub,* etc.). But he wanted to be content at first with obtaining the consonantal "skeleton" which is always the foundation of all understanding in the Semitic languages. Since in following this method, he is bound to come across several signs for the same consonant sound, he transliterates for the time being m_1, m_2, m_3, n_1, n_2, n_3, n_4, etc., hoping to be able some time in the future to replace these notations by *ma, mi, mu, na, ni, nu, an, in, un,* or similar syllables.

Using the letter values *b, š, n* and *t*, obtained from the group of signs presumed to represent a date, Dhorme found the group *n.š* (the delimitation of which as a separate word, however, in either direction is by no means certain!) in the first line of the same inscription, and he believed that it represented the word *nḥš*, "metal, copper," since the text appeared on a copper tablet. With the aid of the knowledge of the sign for *ḥ*, he was able to read the word *mzbḥ*, "altar," in lines 6 and 10, and the knowledge of the *m* in turn enabled him to read, in line 14, before the designation of the year, the designation of a month, viz., $btmz_1$, "in (the month of) Tammuz," containing a second sign for *z*, which he transliterates as z_1. The designations of the month and year can logically be expected to be preceded by the designation of the *day of the month*, written by a *numeral*. The *š.š* is now completed to *šdš*, "six(th)," and the signs following it turned out to be *jm-m*, "day" (with two new signs for *m!*), so that the full date reads: *b-šdš jm-m* $b\text{-}tmz_1$ *b-šnt* 7 = "on the sixth day in (the month of) Tammuz in the year 7."

Untiring work and a constant revision of his findings enabled Dhorme finally to obtain a result which he could present to the Academy of Paris on August 2, 1946. He pointed out that he had searched neither for the name of Byblos nor for the words for "god" or "king," nor for any narrative of conquests or pious deeds, and that the report of an engraver on what he and his co-workers did in decorating the temple had revealed itself to him unbidden. Also the long Tablet *d* revealed a similar content to Dhorme.

Dhorme thus obtained a transliteration of the Proto-Byblic inscriptions, or rather of the consonantal "skeletons" of the words. The missing vowels must still be determined to make the decipherment complete. That should not be a very difficult task, for we are passably familiar with the diachronic picture of the Phoenician vowel system, in word-stems and flexional endings alike. Thus, e.g., a substantive the last consonant of which is *m*, would have to end in *mu* in the nominative singular, in *mi* in the genitive singular, and in *ma* in the accusative singular, etc. For the time being, I am still not sure to what degree or extent it is possible to substitute, as mentioned above, more accurate syllabic values for Dhorme's transliterations, and for this very reason I shall not express any judgment concerning the correctness of his decipherment as yet. Let it remain an open question also whether or not Dhorme's separation of the individual words is correct. At any rate, Dhorme can always support his views by pointing out the fact that his transliterations yield texts that make sense (their graphical, lexical and grammatical features may, of course, still be in need of rectification) as well as the fact that in particular the transliteration of the date of Tablet c which served as his point of departure is corroborated reciprocally by various arguments. Dhorme's decipherment of the Proto-Byblic script is certainly more likely to gain universal recognition than the attempt of Grimme to decipher the Sinaitic writing, which for that very reason I shall discuss later only, among the undeciphered scripts (pp. 159 *et seq.*).

3. The Translation of Other Unknown Languages

For consideration of space, only a few typical examples will be discussed in this section, in order to cast light on the problem as such.

(a) *On the Translation of Etruscan*

The facts that Etruscan has been in the focus of more intense interest than many another language discussed in this book, and that more effort has been expended on its decipherment than on that of the other languages, are indubitably the result of its geographic location in the center of Italy, homeland of an ancient civilization. That land, of such importance in the development of European civilization, seems to have been so strongly under the influence of the Etruscans in the early epoch of its history that a study of the Etruscan language always appeared to be desirable and attractive. The results are, however, by no means commensurate with the efforts devoted to this task; despite the existence of an immense literature dealing with the translation of Etruscan, this author still finds it difficult to state even today whether or not the translation of the language may now be said to have been successfully accomplished. Considerations of space make it absolutely impossible to discuss with any semblance of thoroughness all that has been undertaken in order to unlock the secrets of Etruscan, and the most I can do in this book is to give an outline of a few principal features.

The Etruscan inscriptions known to exist number more than 8,000, the oldest ones of which date back to prior to 600 B.C. Most of them are, however, quite brief, some no more than mere fragments, and chiefly *epitaphs*, consisting usually simply of the name of the deceased and perhaps a brief indication of his age or the public offices held by him. Only a few sarcophagi, such as the sarcophagus of Pulena and that of Alethna, bear longer inscriptions, and only a few inscriptions can be called really long, such as the *tile from S. Maria di Capua*, belonging to the 5th century, with about 300 words on it, and the more recent *Cippus Perusinus* (Perugia *cippus*), with about 120 words. The texts different from the epitaphs are strongly in the minority as for contents, too; let there be mentioned the two leaden *tablets, bearing imprecations* of Volterra and Campiglia Maritima, furthermore the *bronze liver of Piacenza* which once was an instrument of fortune-telling, and also two *dice* on which the numerals from one to six are written out in words. In addition to the "epigraphic" monuments, there are the *linen wrappings* inscribed with a religious text which were found on an Etruscan mummy in the museum of Zagreb in 1892 and have been known to scholars as the "Zagreb mummy wrappings." The more than 1500 words appearing on them constitute the longest Etruscan text known. The small number of longer and thus linguistically more informative Etruscan texts is one of the reasons for the meagerness of the results heretofore achieved by the attempts at the translation of this language.

The texts themselves offer the linguists very little to go by. The known *bilingual inscriptions* consist of just a few quite short and uninformative epitaphs in Latin and Etruscan. For instance, Inscription 378 of the *Corpus Inscriptionum Etruscarum* (= XI 1855 of the *Corpus Inscriptionum Latinarum*) consists of the Etruscan text "V. *Cazi* C. *clan*" and of the Latin phrase "C. *Cassius* C. *f. Saturninus*," the latter meaning "G(aius) Cassius, G(aius') s(on), Saturninus"; hence, the Etruscan word *clan* in the Etruscan portion, in which the name *Saturninus* is missing, means "son," and this meaning is confirmed by other inscriptions. Also isolated translations of Etruscan words occurring in Latin literature, e.g., aisar for "god," furnish only minor help.

The Etruscan glosses accompanying *pictorial representations of subjects from the Greek mythology*, however, do show the Etruscan forms of a number of mythological names, some in an Etruscanized Greek form, as e.g., *Apulu* (Apollo), *Neθuns* (Neptune), *Hercle* (Hercules), *Aχmemrun* (Agamemnon), *Alcsentre* and other variants (Alexander),

Pecse (Pegasus), *Φersipnei* (Persephone), etc., others in Etruscan "translation," as *Tinia* or *Tinš* (Zeus, Jupiter), *Turan* (Venus), *Fufluns* (Dionysos), *Turms* (Mercury), etc. While the first one of these two groups in particular supplies many data concerning Etruscan phonology, these names are hardly of any use to one who tries to gain an insight into the language as a whole.

Thus the only practicable way of translating the inscriptions remains, in the main, to proceed from the inscriptions themselves. Now then, the co-existent use of two distinct methods becomes even more strongly evident in the field of Etruscan than in the translation of other languages, viz.: the *combinatory* method, which seeks to clarify the meaning of the texts on the basis of clues contained in those texts themselves, and the *etymological* method which tries to accomplish the purpose on the strength of phonetic similarities between the language studied and some known language. The possibilities of learning the secrets of Etruscan by the combinatory method are very scant, though. It is understandable therefore why the etymological method has again and again been advocated by various scholars in the study of Etruscan in particular, and why attempts have been made at interpreting this language on the strength of phonetic similarities to the most different languages, such as Basque and Caucasian, Proto-Germanic, Greek and Proto-Indo-European in general, and even Sumerian, to name just a few of the languages selected for this comparison. Above all, individual research linguists would again and again consider Etruscan an Italic language and most closely cognate with Latin and Osco-Umbrian, and they would try to translate it on the ground of its phonetic similarities to these languages, obviously misled by a number of unquestionably Italic loanwords in Etruscan. All these attempts at a translation, often published in bombastic terms, are entirely worthless and tend only to make laymen skeptical about meritorious interpretations of other languages as well.

In the study of Etruscan, the scantiness of the clues makes it especially difficult to make any headway by the combinatory method, which can grope its way forward step by slow step only. It compares, for instance, the bronze liver of Piacenza with similar fortune-telling "livers" of clay used by the Babylonians and the Hittites, and on the strength of this comparison it determines what names of deities appear on the Etruscan liver, which include also *usil*, "sun," and *tiv*, "moon," two appellatives the knowledge of which helps in the clarification of other connections. Thus, the epitaphs often indicate not only the name of the deceased, but also his age in numerals. Therefore, if we find the expression *avils x tivrs y*, we may safely assume that *tiv* meant not only "moon," but also "month," and consequently, *avil* must obviously have meant "year."

Inscriptions appearing on implements and beginning with the word *mi*, followed by names, e.g., *mi Θancvilus Fulnial*, have pointed at the conclusion, based on the analogy of Italic inscriptions on such objects, that *mi* must have meant "this" (possibly also "I") and is to be translated as *this (is)*—respectively *I (am)—Tanaquil Fulnia's*. The circumstance that a woman's name followed by *puia* frequently appears after names of men in the epitaphs, suggests that *puia* must mean "wife." Therefore, *Vel Šeθre puia-c* is translated as "Vel Šethre and (-c) wife," and *Θanxil Ruvfi puia Arnθal Aleθnas* as "Tanaquil Rufia, wife of Arnth Alethna." The words *lupuce* or *svalce* in the statement concerning the age of the deceased are considered as *verbal forms* meaning "(he or she) lived" or "(he or she) died," and *avils LX lupuce* is translated consequently as "he lived 60 years" or "he died (with) 60 years," *svalce avil LXVI* as "he lived 66 years," etc. Accordingly, also the frequently occurring word *amce* (showing the same ending, *-ce*) is regarded as a verbal form and translated as "(he or she) was"; thus, *Ramθa Matulnei* *seχ Marces Matulnal puia-m amce Šeθres Ceisinies* is taken to mean "Ramtha Matulnei was (*amce*) the daughter (*seχ*) of Marcus Matulna, but (*-m*) the wife of Šethre Ceisinie," etc. These few examples demonstrate at least how the combinatory method is able to extract not only lexical meanings but also grammatical rules from the inscriptions.

An entire literature has been written about the six numbers, *θu, zal, ci, śa, maχ, huθ*, appearing on the dice, since they indubitably represent the spoken forms of the numerals from 1 to 6. The only difficult, still not finally solved question is their proper sequence. They were probably arranged similarly to the system used on most ancient dice, so that two opposite numbers always totaled seven, but which of the numbers should be taken to mean "one"? It so happens that also the indications of the age of the deceased in the epitaphs contain numbers written out in letters, namely those mentioned above as well as three more simple numbers, *cezp, semφ* and *nurφ* (which must mean "seven," "eight" and "nine") as well as their derivatives, i.e., tens as *zaθrum* (from *zal*), *cialχ* (from *ci*), *muvalχ* (from *maχ*?), *śealχ* (from *śa*), *cezpalχ* (from *cezp*), *semφalχ* (from *semφ*). The frequency of the occurrence of the tens seems to warrant conclusions as to their numerical values: We may expect 60 and 70 to occur often, but 80 and especially 90 but seldom. However, since the scholars are, as stated before, still not in agreement as to the various details, a mention of this interesting problem must suffice at this place.

Naturally, the "Zagreb mummy wrappings," the longest relic of the Etruscan language, attracted most of the investigators, especially since in 1932 infrared irradiation revealed and permitted to be read also the completely faded portions which had been assumed to be totally illegible. The frequent occurrence of the names of deities indicates that the text is of a religious character, but it differs strongly from the inscriptions both in vocabulary and in phraseology and confronts the combinatory method of research with insurmountable obstacles. Yet, Olzscha succeeded in advancing these studies considerably in 1934–1936. He found that the wrappings had originally constituted a single scroll, several meters in length, and the text had been written on it in columns from right to left. The gaps in the preserved text could be partly filled in because long passages are repeated in the text. This *grouping of the text* was an essential preliminary to Olzscha's conclusions. He established, furthermore, that these analogous portions of the text could be divided into a number of *verse-like units of identical structure*, the arrangement of which recurs regularly in the individual sections. This finding opens up a comprehensive vista of a long, coherent text, whereas formerly only arbitrarily detached pieces could be viewed. The appearance of the name of a deity introducing each verse makes one think of *prayers*. The prayers are separated from each other by short sections which, on the strength of the vocables occurring in them, Olzscha considers ritual directions concerning sacrifices. Directions for sacrifices and prayers are found to alternate similarly on the *Iguvine Tables*, the longest document extant in the Umbrian language, and similar Roman prayers are contained finally in Cato's treatise *de re rustica*. Although the Umbrian and Roman prayers do not exactly blend with the Etruscan ones so as to form what we could consider a "bilingual record," they still constitute close parallels to them and can be used, with proper caution, in the translation of the Etruscan text of the mummy wrappings. At any rate, they encouraged Olzscha to undertake a new, complete translation of this peculiar literary relic of the Etruscan language. I do not propose to claim that he found the right answer in each and every particular, yet his work seems to have opened up a new inroad into this heretofore so unyielding language.

Let us hope that future research will be able to solve also the enigma of the linguistic affinities of this language which today still stands isolated. Recent discoveries disprove Herbig's theory of a close affinity between Etruscan and Lydian.* In the opinion of this author, though, also Olzscha is mistaken in considering Etruscan a cognate language of Urartaean.

(b) *On the Translation of Other Languages of Ancient Italy*

After the preceding discussion of Etruscan, a short glance at the translation of ancient Italic languages in general does not seem to be out of place.

The credit for the translation of *Osco-Umbrian*, the closest relative of Latin among the Indo-European languages of ancient Italy, is due chiefly to the linguistic science of the 19th century. This is a domain where the etymological method appears to be not only permissible, but in fact the only one that can be expected to produce a result. The reason is that Osco-Umbrian is almost as close to Latin as Dutch is to German; not only have the two languages very many words and grammatical features in common, but with a similarity of all phases of communal and private life, also the style and phraseology of the inscriptions parallel each other completely. Let this be demonstrated by the following specimen of an Oscan inscription from Pompeii which I accompany here also by its Latin translation in order to make especially evident the close parallel of the two languages:

* Cf. p. 109.

[OSCAN]—(1) V. *Aadirans* V. *eítiuvam paam* (2) *vereiiaí Púmpaiianaí trístaa-* (3) *mentud deded eísak eítiuvad* (4) V. *Viínikiís Mr. kvaísstur Púmp-* (5) *aiians tríībúm ekak kúmben-* (6) *nieís tanginud úpsannam* (7) *deded ísídum* prúfatted.

[LATIN TRANSLATION]—(1) V. Adiranus V. (filius) pecuniam quam (2) iuventuti Pompeianae testa- (3) mento dedit, ea pecunia (4) V. Vinicius Mr. (filius) quaestor Pom- (5) peianus domum hanc conven- (6) tus sententia faciendam (7) dedit, idem probavit.

[ENGLISH TRANSLATION]—(1) Which money V(ibius) Adiranus (son of) V(ibius), (2) to the youth of Pompeii by testa- (3) ment did give, from that money (4) did V(ibius) Vinicius, (son of) M(ara), quaestor of Pompeii, (5) this house according to the meet- (6) ing's decision to be built (7) caused; he approved (it).

Whereas Latin and Osco-Umbrian are close linguistic relatives and their speakers shared the same culture, the situation is quite different with respect to the language of the *Veneti* of northeastern Italy. Venetic is not just an Italic dialect, but perhaps a separate branch of Indo-European which does have features in common with Italic, but also with Celtic, Germanic and Illyrian. A clear insight into the Venetic language is impeded by the fact that the entire linguistic legacy of the Veneti consists of a number of brief inscriptions on utensils and tools which follow more or less the same pattern, viz., "I (am) X's (tool)" or "X presented me to Y."

In the course of the translation of the Venetic inscription *eχo Voltiχeneh vesoś*, the meaning of *eχo* is determined, of course, etymologically on the basis of its phonetic similarity to the Latin *ego*, etc. ("I"); this conclusion, however, is influenced not only by that phonetic similarity but also by the objective, combinatory consideration that inscriptions on tools found also in other regions of Italy and the Old World usually begin with "I" and are phrased as if the tool itself were speaking. The same objective consideration applies when the Venetic inscription *meχo Vhuχiia zonasto Rehtiiah* is translated etymologically as "me (*meχo*) presented (*zonasto*) Vhuχia to Rehtia." The words *eχo* and *meχo* remind the translator of the German *ich* and *mich* (*I* and *me*), rather than of the Latin *ego* and *me;* the word *zonasto* is a Greek-style s-aorist of the verbal stem *zona-* = Latin *dona-re,* "to present." In these cases, therefore, the translation is not obtained by the method of phonetic analogy alone, but by the *etymological method, supported by objective, combinatory considerations.*

Whereas this sort of etymological interpretation still moves more or less on firm soil, the following example leads one easily onto the territory of hypotheses. *Ancient* Calabria in the extreme southeast of Italy (between Brindisi and Taranto—not identical with modern Calabria opposite Sicily)—was inhabited once by the *Messapians* who spoke an Indo-European language, cognate perhaps with Illyrian, preserved in a number of brief inscriptions as well as two longer ones. One of them, found in the city of Basta, begins with the words *θotoria marta pido vastei basta veinan aran,* which Krahe translates as "Tutoria Marta /a woman's name/ handed over /= sold?; *pido*/ to the city (*vastei*) /of/ Basta her (*veinan*) field (*aran*)." He considers *vastei* the dative singular of a word cognate with the Greek *ástu,* "city"; he looks at *pido* as a verbal form, taken to be a root aorist, *(e)*pi-dō-t,* "gave over," from the Indo-European root **dō-* in the Greek *dí-dō-mi,* "I give"; he regards *ara-* as a substantive belonging to the Latin *arare* ("to plough") and meaning "field" (like the Latvian *ara* for "field"), whereas he sees *veina-* as a possessive pronoun, "his," derived from the Indo-

European *su̯eino- and identified with the Gothic *seina-* and the German *sein.* The impression gained here by an unbiased observer is that the translation of the words is based on the phonetic similarities alone, without sufficient objective clues, and that this translation *may* but not necessarily *must* be right. For instance, von Blumenthal translated the same phrase, breaking it into words somewhat differently, *θotoria marta pidova steibasta veinan aran,* as "The dead (*marta*) Tutoria bequeathed her field by a testament" /considering *pidova* the instrumental of *(e)*pi-dovā-,* "surrender," and *steibasta* an s-aorist of a verb analogous with the Latin *stipulari,* "to have something stipulated." This example demonstrates how the etymological method can lead to different results by different interpretations, and how both results and interpretations can still claim a certain degree of plausibility. But only one of them can be right at best, and all of them may be wrong. This uncertainty is all the more unpleasant because Krahe makes use of this very interpretation for a foundation on which to build such important comparative-linguistic conclusions as the analogy of the formation of the pronouns *my, your, his* in Messapian and the Germanic languages. It should be very understandable that this author cannot conceal his scruples about such a far-reaching etymological interpretation.

(c) *On the Translation of Phrygian*

In contrast to the linguistic disunity of ancient Italy where a number of closely related Italic and more remotely cognate Indo-European languages as well as the non-Indo-European Etruscan were spoken, Greece was a closed linguistic unit, for even though its inhabitants spoke several distinct dialects, those were still dialects of one and the same language. We find no parallel in the Greek speech area, above all, to the relationship between Latin and Osco-Umbrian. But there is at least one language which investigators have considered more closely related to Greek and to a certain extent also interpreted etymologically on the basis of Greek, viz.: the language of the *Phrygians* who lived in the interior of Asia Minor. The Phrygian language has been preserved in about twenty-five *Old Phrygian* inscriptions, written about the 7th–6th centuries B.C., with a slightly modified variant of the Greek alphabet, and in nearly 100 *Neo-Phrygian* inscriptions, originating from the era of the Roman Empire and written in standard Greek characters. But Neo-Phrygian was only occasionally used as the language of an entire inscription; generally, the inscription is written in Greek, with an imprecatory formula added to it in Neo-Phrygian.

This imprecatory formula is also the only Phrygian text which we understand with any degreee of certainty. In this connection, we might even speak of a kind of bilingual record, inasmuch as the average wording of the Neo-Phrygian imprecatory formula, *ios ni semoun knoumanei kakoun addaket etittetikmenos eitou* corresponds to the occasionally encountered Greek formula, τὶς δὲ ταύτηι ϑαλάμειν κακὸν ποσ-ποιήσει κατηραμένος ἤτω, i.e., "but whoever will inflict evil to this sepulchral chamber, shall be accursed." Accordingly, the Phrygian words can be interpreted as follows: *ios* = a relative pronoun (Indo-European **i̯o-s*, Greek *hos*); *ni* = an emphatic particle added to that pronoun; *semou*(n) = dative singular of the masculine and neuter form of the demonstrative pronoun meaning "this" (Indo-European **ki-* and **ko-*, Slavic *si-* with the masculine-neuter dative singular *semu*, etc.); *knouman* = "grave" or "monument on a grave"; *kakoun* = "evil" (loan-word from the Greek *kakós*, "evil," or originally cognate with this word, unknown in other Indo-European languages?); *ad-daket* = "he inflicts" (*ad* = Latin ad, "to"; *daket* = "he places, puts," cf. Greek tí-thē-mi, "I lay, place," aorist *é-thē-ka*); *eti-ttetikmenos* =

"accursed" (passive perfect participle ending in *-menos* as in Greek, in which connection again it is an open question whether this identical ending is to be ascribed to linguistic borrowing or to original cognateness); *eitou* = "he shall be" (Greek *éstō*) or "he shall go" (Greek *ítō*)?

The interpretation of the imprecatory formula is feasible also without the etymological method. Also the Old Phrygian inscription *ates* | *arkiaevais* | *akenanolavos* | *midai* | *lavaltaei* | *vanaktei* | *edaes*, written clearly and with the words separated from each other, appears to be more or less clearly understandable as "Ates, (son) of Arkiaevis (?) ...... placed (it) for Midas Lavaltas, the prince," but the etymological method is still not completely eliminated in the translation of *vanaktei*, "to the prince" /Greek (*v*)*anax*, "prince"/ and of the verbal form *edaes*, "he placed" /s-aorist of the root **dhē-* in the Greek *tí-thē-mi*, "I place"; Hittite *dāiš*, "he placed"/.

The combinatory method is all too often compelled to admit its own incompetency when it is applied to longer inscriptions, more ancient or more recent ones alike, especially when the words are run together without any indication of where one word ends and another one begins, which is the method usually observed in the Neo-Phrygian texts, and encountered in some Old Phrygian inscriptions as well. In such cases, the etymological interpretation based on phonetic and morphological analogies with other Indo-European languages has become more or less the standard procedure. The investigators who apply it can cite precedents, viz., the translation by the etymological method of Old Persian on the basis of the cognate Sanskrit language, or that of the Osco-Umbrian inscriptions with the aid of the knowledge of Latin. As to details, though, opinions diverge no less widely than in the instance of the Messapian inscription cited as an example on page 145. For instance, the word-group *attiadei-*

tou appearing in the Neo-Phrygian phrase *etittetikmenos attiadeitou* (in which the word *etittetikmenos* is known, as explained above, to mean "accursed") is broken up by some linguists as *Atti ad-eitou*, "he shall hurry to (the god) Attis" (*ad-eitou* = Latin *ad-ito* = "he shall hurry to"), but by others as *at Tiad eitou*, "he shall go to Zeus" (*at* = Latin *ad* = "to"; *Tiad* for **Tian-de* = "to Zeus"), so that the former translate the phrase as "accursed, he shall hurry to Attis," but the latter as "accursed, he shall go to Zeus." As a second example, I mention the Neo-Phrygian word group *otuvoivetei* which R. Meister breaks into the two words *otuvoi vetei* and translates as "in the eighth year," assuming that *vetei* = the Greek (*v*)*étos* = "year," and *otuvoi* = the Latin *octavus* = "eighth" (with a change of the *-ct-* by assimilation to *-t*(*t*)-, analogously to the Italian *otto* < Latin octo, "eight"). But O. Haas breaks the same group into three words, *Otu voi vetei*, and he translates them as "Otys to his (*voi*) relatives (Greek *étēs*)."

R. Meister, in particular, went to extremes in translating Phrygian on the basis of Greek analogies. He evidently regarded the Phrygian language as a strongly altered dialect of Greek. Let his method be illustrated on two sentences from the Old Phrygian inscriptions appearing on the tomb of Arezastis: *zostututa?i?* | *a?e?mnoz?* | *akenanolavos*, translated as "who is begotten from the blood of Akenanolas," viz.: *zos* = a relative pronoun (= Greek *hos*); *tututai* (?) for **tétuktai* from the Greek *teuchō*, "I create"; *aemnoz* (?) = genitive for ablative singular from the Greek *haĩma*, "blood." The second sentence is the artist's note (?) appearing at the end: *ataniz en* | *kurzanezon* | *tane lertoz*, "Atanis chiselled this in the Gordian's (territory)," viz.: *lertōz* = "he chiselled," on the analogy of the Greek *(e)*lértōse*; *tane* = "this" (Greek *tá-de*); *Kurzanēzōn* = genitive plural of an adjective of citizenship derived from the name of the city of Gordion.

But also the other investigators have not yet succeeded in achieving any unambiguous and convincing explanation of the Phrygian inscriptions. While O. Haas does not follow one-sidedly the method of translating on the basis of Greek analogies, even he proceeds very arbitrarily in the separation of words and in his etymological interpretations, and in most cases he fails to produce proof of the latter. Thus, *diounsin* is interpreted, without any objective proof, as "the living one" and traced back to the Indo-European **gu̯i-i̯ont-si-n*, but at the same time also *augoi* is translated as "living" and explained as a derivative of **āi̯ugoi* (from Old Indic *āyu-*, "life"). The word *argousi* is called a loan form of the Greek *árchousi*, "(at) the archons," and the word *isgeiket* a loan form of the Greek *eíschēke*, "he has received." This ought to suffice to demonstrate that the translation of Phrygian is still very much in its infancy, and that the general public will still be wise to regard it with a little skepticism.

III. PRINCIPLES OF THE METHODOLOGY OF THE DECIPHERMENT OF EXTINCT SCRIPTS AND LANGUAGES

Now that we have become acquainted with quite a number of decipherments, we are in the position to derive from them a series of basic principles relative to the decipherment of unknown scripts and languages in general. These basic considerations could have been presented at the beginning of this book as well, but if the uninitiated layman had met them there, they might easily have impressed him as somewhat dry and abstract, whereas given here, they represent a practical summary of the facts elucidated on the preceding pages, and thus they might not be entirely without value for future decipherments either.

To begin with, I must state once again the fact, self-evident and trite as it may be, that the decipherment of any unknown script or language presupposes the availability of some clue or reference; *nothing can be deciphered out of nothing.* In those cases where one has absolutely no possibility available to link the unknown to something known, the amateur can give free rein to his imagination, but no real or lasting result can be accomplished.

Furthermore, we must distinguish three different types of decipherment, which at the same time represent three different degrees of difficulty. The task at hand may comprise the *translation of an unknown language written in a known script,* as in the cases of cuneiform Hittite and Etruscan, or *the language may be a known one but written in an unknown script,* like Cypriote Greek, and finally, there are cases involving *an unknown language written in a likewise unknown script.* The last variant of the problem is, of course, the most difficult one. This is why, for instance, the translation of cuneiform Hittite cannot be considered being on the same level with the decipherment of the Egyptian hieroglyphics or of cuneiform writing in general.

When some *unknown script* is to be deciphered, a number of preliminary questions of fundamental importance can be clarified in most cases even before the real work is begun. The *direction of the writing* can be recognized in most instances by the position of the blank end of the last line of the inscription (cf. the Hittite hieroglyphic inscription shown in Fig. 39 and the inscription written bilingually in Phoenician and Cypriote, shown in Fig. 60). The decipherer can decide whether or not the *words are separated* by systematically recurring strokes, periods, colons, or other similar signs, and he can draw conclusions as to the difficulty of the decipherment accordingly.

Above all, the *number of the written symbols* usually warrants a conclusion as to whether the script is alphabetic, a pure syllabary (as in the Cypriote) or a mixture of ideographic word-signs and syllabic signs (like the cuneiform writing or the Hittite hieroglyphic script). A script consisting of less than thirty signs will presumably turn out to be alphabetic; the probability of its decipherment is higher than that of a more complicated system. Scripts containing fifty, a hundred, or even several hundred different symbols may justifiably be regarded beforehand as more or less complicated syllabic systems of writing, perhaps employing also word-signs, and their decipherment can be expected to involve more considerable difficulties. It was decided rather accurately, even before the decipherment of one single cuneiform character, that the trilingual inscriptions of the early

Persian kings consisted of three parallel versions, one (the Old Persian text) written in an alphabetic script, a second one (the Neo-Elamite version) couched in syllabic symbols, and a third (the Akkadian) one presumably written with ideographic word-signs.

The decipherment proper is facilitated most by a *bilingual text* ("*bilinguis*"), i.e., an inscription in which the text written in the unknown language or script is followed or preceded by its translation in some known language or script. The preceding discussions of the various decipherments demonstrate that such bilingual texts (in fact, even some *trilingual texts,* i.e., *trilinguis*) are fortunately available often enough. Neither the Egyptian hieroglyphics nor the Babylonian cuneiform writing could have been deciphered without a bilingual text, and the Hittite hieroglyphic writing is the sole instance where the unknown script, and partly also the language, was deciphered without the aid of a bilingual text and the decipherment was later confirmed by a subsequently discovered bilingual text.

Regardless of which of the three types of decipherment is involved, the decipherer will first be on the lookout for *names* of persons, cities, countries, etc. in the known portion of the bilingual text and then try to find their equivalents in the unknown part. A prerequisite of this procedure is that the names actually be identical or similar in the two versions, and in most instances they are, too. The rare case that some name is entirely different in the two versions (cf. Italian *Ragusa* = Croatian *Dubrovnik*) occurs also in the languages of the ancient Orient, for instance, the Urartaean city *Ardini* was called *Muṣaṣir* in Akkadian. The decipherer finds corroborative evidence of the correctness of his way of reading the written symbols in particular in the favorable case when the same written symbol occurs more than once in the same name or in more than one name; I mentioned the hieroglyphic Hittite names *Tuwanuwa*, *Gurguma* and *Amatu* (cf. pp. 92 *et seq.*). Names are the most important, often the only means of gaining the first foothold in the field of the reading of an unknown script; but they are important also when the problem at hand is purely one of linguistic interpretation, because they are instrumental in the grouping of the words which in turn is valuable with respect to the translation of words and the determination of their grammatical functions. Besides the names, the titles are important, as in phrases like, e.g., "X, king of the land of Y," etc.

In the absence of bilingual texts, the decipherers look for other media of help. I mentioned above (p. 53) how Grotefend had made good use of his knowledge of the names of the Early Persian kings as recorded by Herodotus to open up a way to the understanding of the Early Persian royal inscriptions, and what an important part was played in that connection by the fact that Hystaspes, the father of Darius, had been no king. And the mention of the names of North Syrian cities and their rulers in the war reports of Assyrian kings was helpful in the first groping attempts at the reading of Hittite hieroglyphic inscriptions. Legends on tools, suspected to mean "(Ax of) Y" or "This is the tool of Y," were valuable in the decipherment of the Ugaritic script as well as in the translation of Etruscan. The clues which permit one to make headway in the unravelling of the secrets of extinct languages and scripts are quite varied and cannot be classified under rigid, inflexible rules. The detection and exploitation of these possibilities depends chiefly on the individual skill of the decipherer, and every project of decipherment may present new surprises in this respect. It may, however, happen also that no point of attack can be found at all and all the efforts of the decipherer are in vain.

When the problem at hand is *to translate an unknown language* written in the *cuneiform characters* deciphered about a century ago, the investigator is in a particularly favorable position because cuneiform writing itself paves the way to its understanding by making use of a combination of different scriptural elements, i.e., ideograms, syllabic symbols and determinatives. If an Assyriologist who knows only Akkadian looks at a cuneiform Hittite or Urartaean text, he will immediately recognize a number of familiar elements, chiefly in the ideograms and determinatives. The determinatives will enable him, even without knowing the language of the inscription, immediately to classify certain words as names of men or women, of gods or goddesses, geographical names, names of professions, etc.; the ideograms will enable him to recognize inflectional (declensional or conjugational, as the case may be) endings, from which he can draw conclusions to help him both in the translation of an individual inscription and in the recognition of general grammatical facts. The great extent of the aid rendered by the ideograms and determinatives in cuneiform writing can be properly appreciated only by one who has personally attempted to contribute to the understanding of a language written in cuneiform characters as well as of another language written in a different script, say Lydian or Etruscan. In the language written in cuneiform characters, a number of linguistic facts become immediately evident; on the other hand, uncertainty continues to prevail even about the most simple questions, such as whether a given word is a proper name or a common noun. Also the Lycian text on the Stela of Xanthos (cf. p. 104) would be easier to translate if the script had included determinatives, etc., to facilitate its understanding by the reader.

One must always try to interpret an unknown language, whether written in cuneiform script or by some other system of writing, by the *combinatory* method, i.e., on the ground of objective clues and conclusions. This is, of course, often a difficult undertaking when the unknown language is not written with cuneiform characters, especially when the number of available inscriptions and records of the language is small, or when the texts are particularly brief and uninformative. It is therefore psychologically comprehensible, and yet methodologically wrong, that, e.g., Etruscologists were all too willing to be guided by phonetical coincidences and attempted to translate unknown words *etymologically* according to the meaning of similarly sounding words in known languages. I can never warn my readers too often or too emphatically against this procedure, for its basic principle is as if one wanted to translate the Latin *laus*, "praise," on the ground of its assonance with the German *Laus* or the English *louse*, or the Central American Mayan word *catz*, "poultry," on the analogy of the English *cats*, or the modern Greek *nay*, "yes," on the analogy of the English dialectal *nay* (meaning *no*). The etymological method is permissible to a certain extent when applied to *closely related languages*, but even in those cases it must go hand in hand *with objective considerations*. And phonetic similarity plays tricks even in the cases of closely related languages: The German *Gift* means "poison," and the German verb *bekommen* does not mean "to become," but "to receive." In any case, the explorer of an unknown language must never declare flatly that "*Words that sound alike or similar in two languages, mean the same thing in both*," but he must endeavor to present objective arguments at least to support any such conclusion based on a phonetic similarity.

It is, of course, especially difficult, and in many cases practically impossible, *to decipher an unknown script without the aid of a bilingual text* containing names. Many a failure to accomplish the decipherment of some writing is directly attributable to the lack of bilingual inscriptions or other references. But the possibility of deciphering a script without bilingual texts, too, is demonstrated by the example of the Hittite hieroglyphic writing. Thus, it might be more prudent to say when discussing a script which has defied all attempts to decipher it, that science has not yet been fortunate enough to discover a suitable point of departure for the decipherment. This principle is another conclusion warranted by a study of the earlier and later stages of the decipherment of the Hittite hieroglyphics.

Combinatory methods are the proper procedure in the decipherment of scripts, too, but this is another instance where the proper procedure has not always been duly followed. As the amateur is all too prone to declare in the *translation of a language* that "Whatever *sounds* alike or similar, also means the same thing," in the *decipherment of a script* people are likely to commit the methodological error of stating that "Whatever *looks* similar in two scripts, means the same thing." Thus, Hrozný committed a fundamental error in his attempts to decipher the Cretan-Minoan writing (cf. p. 165) as well as when trying to decipher the Indus Valley script (cf. p. 170), viz., he tried to determine the meanings or values of the unknown characters on the ground of indiscriminately applied analogies with symbols of similar (and occasionally not even similar) appearance of the Hittite hieroglyphic script, but also of the South Arabian and other scripts. This is the same amateurish method which is applied by a layman completely ignorant of Russian writing who looks for the first time at a Russian text and sees in it a number of familiar characters, fully identical with the corresponding letters of the Roman alphabet, such as A, K, M, O, etc., and is therefore convinced that also the Russian P (read as our R) stands for the Roman P, the Russian C (read as our S) for the Roman C, the Russian H (read as our N) for the Roman H, etc. This error is pardonable in a layman, but it should not be committed by a scholarly investigator. The fundamental question whether the Indus Valley script is an alphabetic, syllabic or ideographic writing, is not raised by Hrozný at all. Future decipherers ought by all means to guard against such basic errors.

IV. A FEW EXAMPLES OF UNDECIPHERED SCRIPTS

I HAVE stated (p. 157) that many a failure to decipher a given script is attributable to the simple fact that the investigators have not yet discovered the suitable point of departure. In conclusion of the present book, I shall present a few examples of such unsuccessful attempts to decipher unknown scripts, but these are merely examples, without any claim to completeness. Occasionally I shall be in the position also to point out a few facts which may explain *why* it has been impossible to accomplish the decipherment as yet.

1. The Sinaitic Script

I include the so-called Sinaitic script, even at the risk of exposing myself to contradiction, among those writings the decipherment of which still has not been accomplished. This script has been preserved in a few brief inscriptions, discovered by Flinders Petrie, an archeologist, in the ancient copper and malachite mines of Mount Sinai, particularly near the ruins of a temple of the Egyptian goddess Hathor, in the winter of 1904–1905; Petrie determined, on archeological grounds, that the inscriptions had been made about 1500 B.C. The very carelessly and disuniformly written signs look partly like Egyptian hieroglyphics, but there are not more than thirty-two distinguishable individual signs, so that it is quite logical to suspect that they are the symbols of an alphabetic system. We are, however, still so uncertain about the shapes of the individual symbols that it is often doubtful whether two signs of very similar appearance are to be regarded as two different signs or as variants of one and the same character. After all, we do know an alphabetic script consisting of characters closely resembling those of the Egyptian writing, viz., the Meroitic script (cf. pp. 26 *et seq.*), although it is true that the Meroitic characters originated much later, in the Roman era.

The British Egyptologist Gardiner worked on these inscriptions during World War I. Since it was impossible to read them on the basis of Egyptian ideographic and phonetic signs, and because a few signs resembled early Semitic letters, Gardiner assumed that this script might represent a preliminary stage to Semitic alphabetic writing, more exactly a link between Egyptian hieroglyphics and the Semitic alphabetic system. In other words, he fell into the error mentioned above (cf. p. 159) of letting himself be guided by similarities in shape and appearance, and despite the mutilated state of the inscriptions, he felt justified in reading the group of symbols shown in Fig. 63 as the Semitic *b'lt*, "lady," and interpreting it as a Semitic designation of the Egyptian

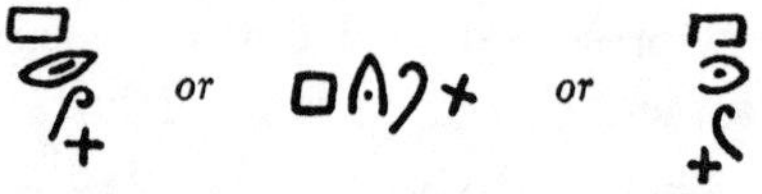

Fig. 63. Alleged *Ba'alat* in Sinaitic script. (From Jensen, *Die Schrift*, Fig. 183.)

goddess Hathor. Gardiner's theory was that the creators of this script had proceeded as follows: They took over the Egyptian symbol (*pr* = house) in the shape of , but since the Semitic word for "house" was *baith* (*bēth*), they

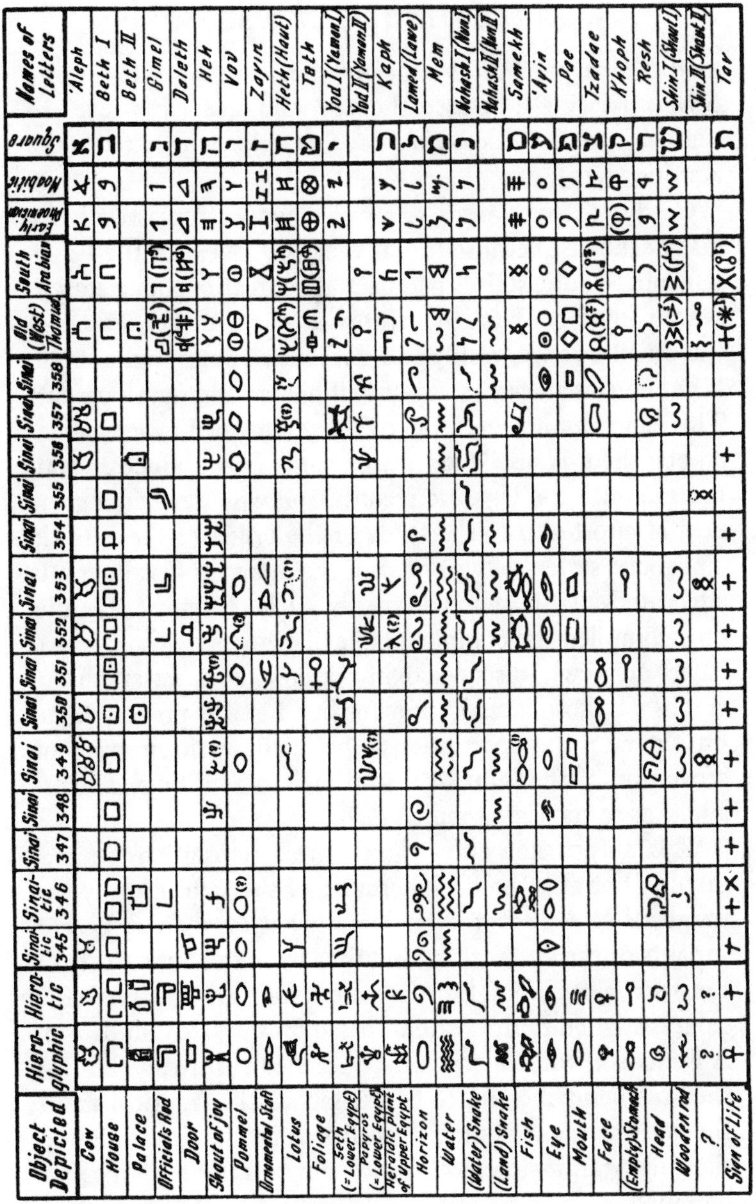
Object Depicted
Hieroglyphic
Hieratic
Sinaitic 345
Sinaitic 346
Sinai 347
Sinai 348
Sinai 349
Sinai 350
Sinai 351
Sinai 352
Sinai 353
Sinai 354
Sinai 355
Sinai 356
Sinai 357
Sinai 358
Old (West) Thamud
South Arabian
Early Phoenician
Moabitic
Square
Names of Letters
Cow
House
Palace
Official's Rod
Door
Shout of joy
Pommel
Ornamental Staff
Lotus
Foliage
Seth (=Lower Egypt)
Papyros (=Lower Egypt)
Heraldic plant of Upper Egypt
Horizon
Water
(Water) Snake
(Land) Snake
Fish
Eye
Mouth
Face
(Empty) Stomach
Head
Wooden rod
?
Sign of Life
'Aleph
Beth I
Beth II
Gimel
Daleth
Heh
Vov
Zayin
Heth (Haut)
Tath
Yod I (Yamen I)
Yod II (Yamen II)
Kaph
Lamed (Lawe)
Mem
Nahash I (Nun I)
Nahash II (Nun II)
Samekh
'Ayin
Pae
Tzadae
Khoph
Resh
Shin I (Shaut I)
Shin II (Shaut II)
Tav

FIG. 64. Table of the signs of the Sinaitic script. (From Jensen, *Die Schrift*, Fig. 187.)

used it as a phonetic symbol of the letter *b* (the Semitic *bēth*); likewise, they used the Egyptian 𓁹 (*jrt* = eye) to represent the Semitic *ʻayin* = eye, as well as the letter *ʻ* (the Semitic *ʻayin*), etc.

Gardiner's hypothesis was welcomed enthusiastically by many scholars, because the missing link between the Egyptian and Semitic scripts had been the target of a long search. Also many a book on the history of our alphabet discussed the Sinaitic script, rashly and without scruples, right at the beginning, as an early stage of that history and development. This view was, however, opposed by renowned investigators, among them Hans Bauer, whose name I mentioned in connection with the Ugaritic records, and who devoted a great deal of effort also to the study of the origin of the Semitic alphabetic system of writing. But the theory of Gardiner was advocated all the more decidedly by H. Grimme. He not only compiled the complete table of signs shown in Fig. 64, based on newly discovered inscriptions and better photographs of those already known, but he also proceeded to transliterate the inscriptions (originally written without separation of the individual words) into Semitic characters and thus to translate them.

This author not only regards these translations as premature, but also the decipherment of the signs as fully unfounded. We do not even know what symbols represent variants of the same letter, and thus we are not at all sure of the very number of the characters, nor are the phonetic values assigned to the symbols based on any safe foundation. A firmer soil will conceivably be reached eventually, but for the time being it seems to be advisable to be skeptical about the decipherment as such, as well as about its application in drawing grammatological conclusions of far-reaching importance.

2. The Cretan-Minoan Script

No success has been accomplished as yet in the decipherment of the different systems of writing discovered on the island of Crete as witnesses to its pre-Greek culture.* The overall view of the development of writing in Crete is complicated in that we know a Cretan *pictographic* writing used on stone seals in a primitive and in a more advanced stage (about 2000–1600 B.C.), consisting of about 140 signs (cf. Fig. 65), and *two linear scripts*, preserved on clay tablets and seals, designated *Linear Class A* and *Linear Class B*, respectively. Linear Class A, consisting of 85 signs (cf. Fig. 66), is

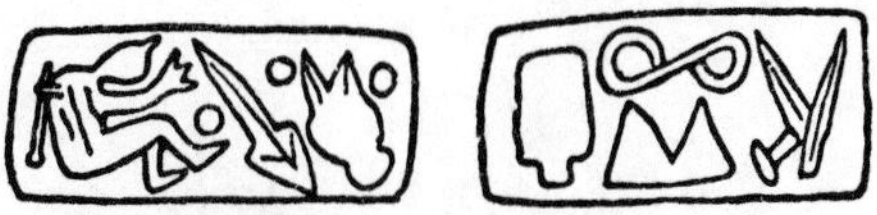

Fig. 65. Cretan pictographic writing. (From Jensen, *Die Schrift*, Fig. 75.)

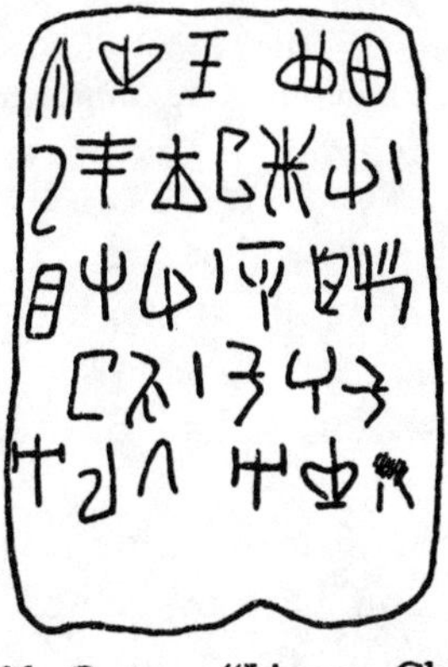

Fig. 66. Cretan "Linear Class A." (From Jensen, *Die Schrift*, Fig. 79.)

* For the latest developments, see Appendix, p. 175.

not restricted to any specific part of the island, whereas Linear Class B (cf. Fig. 67), the symbols of which number 73, is found only in one part of Crete, viz., in Knossos, but inscriptions in Linear Class B have been found also in Pylos, on the Greek mainland. We know vessels found in Thebes,

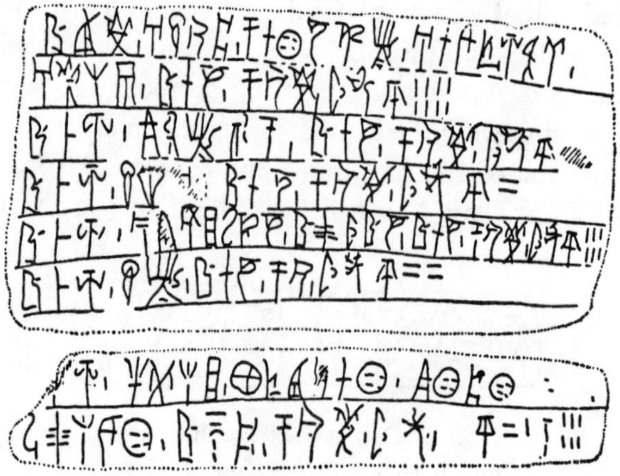

FIG. 67. Two inscriptions, from Pylos, in Cretan-Minoan Linear Script B. (From Peruzzi, *Aportaciones a la interpretación de los textos minoicos*, p. 80.)

Orchomenos, Eleusis and Tiryns, inscribed with symbols of special forms which may well be called *Linear Class C*. Since pictographic symbols are of a minor importance in attempts at decipherment, the term "Cretan script" is generally used to designate Linear Classes A or B, unless expressly stated otherwise.

The decipherment of these inscriptions is still in its initial stage. I shall mention here by name only two especially capable scholars specializing in this field: The indefatigable Johannes Sundwall of Finland, and the American Alice Kober who unfortunately died so very young. They painstakingly collected the different signs, investigated their occurrence individually or in groups, and then they made careful attempts to determine their character, whether ideograms or syllabic signs, but still without trying to read them, for the time is still not ripe for taking that important step.

The more impetuous investigators are not satisfied by this progress. In particular, Hrozný, who had successfully laid the foundations for cuneiform Hittite research and then worked, even though with questionable success, on the hieroglyphic Hittite records, felt qualified for reading the Cretan script, too. Unfortunately, he resorted to a method which I decried as amateurish (cf. p. 157), viz., he compared the Cretan symbols to Hittite hieroglyphics of similar appearance and simply assigned the Hittite phonetic values to the Cretan characters. In addition to the Hittite hieroglyphics, he made use, to a lesser extent, also of the Egyptian hieroglyphics as well as of the South Arabian and other scripts to determine the phonetic values of the Cretan symbols. Unfortunately, all these efforts, undertaken at such great expenditure on reproducing Cretan symbols in print, etc., are mere flights of fancy which are devoid of all objective foundation. Not only all the readings of geographic names and names of deities are to be regarded as fictitious, but so are also all the conclusions concerning linguistic features common to Cretan and hieroglyphic Hittite.

Sittig's "decipherment of the oldest syllabic writing of Europe" is based on more serious and objective considerations than the work of Hrozný. Sittig investigates the structure of the language statistically and compares, above all, the initial and final sounds of Cretan words with those of the non-Greek Cypriote language, for the two languages and scripts were suspected in the past to be related. Sittig reasons that if a Cretan symbol is used structurally exactly like a graphically similar symbol of the Cypriote script (i.e., if both appear, for instance, only at the beginning of a word or never as the final symbol of a word, etc.), he is justified to regard the two symbols as representing the same sound, too. Thus, after laborious preliminary studies, he finally ends up once again with the comparison of the external shapes of signs, which is a very deceptive foundation. In his attempts at reading entire texts, he does not use Cretan tablets, but inscriptions from Greece, in which he tries to identify the Greek language. Whatever he thus reads out of—or into—the inscriptions, is partly Etruscan (Tyrrhenian) and partly Greek, but the latter language does by no means always appear in the form to be expected according to the teachings of diachronic linguistics. But aside from these facts, the salient point is in my opinion that it is wrong and misleading simply to take the attitude that *graphically* similar Cretan and Cypriote signs represent the same *sound*, disregarding weighty statistical data. This author is therefore justified in calling also Sittig's attempt at a decipherment unsuccessful.

Among the scriptorial relics of Crete mention must be made, finally, of the *Phaistos Disk*, a clay tablet found in the fortress of Phaistos in 1908. It is covered with pictographic symbols which are arranged in distinctly separated groups and are unlike any symbols known from Crete or anywhere else. A frequently occurring character is the likeness of a human head with a plumed head-dress which reminds the observer of Asia Minor, so that it has been conjectured that this isolated relic (Fig. 68) was imported from southwestern Asia Minor. Also this isolated and relatively brief text cannot be deciphered without points of reference. Nevertheless, the decipherment has been attempted several times in this case, too, but always unsuccessfully, even though some attempts—like the most recent one by E. Schertel—donned the scientific trappings of a *mathematical method*, operating with frequency curves for the various symbols. Schertel claims that the inscription on the disc is in an Indo-European

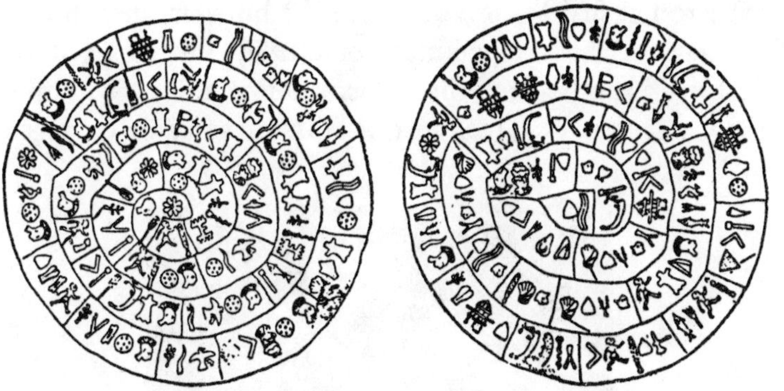

FIG. 68. The Phaistos Disk. (From Diringer, *The Alphabet*. Fig 40.

language closely cognate with Latin, written in a mixture of syllabic and alphabetic writing, and that the text is a double hymn to Zeus and the Minotaur. These numerous positive findings are in striking (and for that very reason suspicious) contrast to the meager results gained from the Cretan texts by Johannes Sundwall and Alice Kober. At any rate, however, those meager results are the more trustworthy ones.

3. The Carian Script

The script and language of ancient Caria (a province in southwestern Asia Minor, between Lydia and Lycia) are another enigma that still continues to baffle investigators. The known Carian inscriptions now number almost one hundred, but most of them are quite short. For a long time, only very few texts found in Caria itself were known, and the bulk of the known Carian records consisted of short scrawls left in Egypt by Carian mercenaries, often very unclearly scribbled and also not always faithfully reproduced in the publications. More recently, however, the number of inscriptions discovered in Caria proper has been increasing; in fact, three of them contain Carian and Greek texts and were expected at first to turn out to be the bilingual inscriptions needed for the decipherment of Carian. But closer study destroyed this hope; in these inscriptions (cf. Fig. 69) either the Carian or the Greek text or both are so badly damaged

FIG. 69. Inscription in Greek and Carian. (From Robert Hellenica VIII, Table II.)

that it has still been impossible to identify the Carian equivalents of the names appearing in the Greek texts. Thus, even if these bilingual inscriptions did consist of Carian and Greek versions of the same text, they still remain useless for the decipherment of Carian for the time being.

Nor are there any other clues available now to permit any progress in the decipherment. The uncertainty is increased by the circumstance that there is often nothing to indicate where a word ends and another word begins, even in the only longer inscription extant, that of Kaunos (Fig. 70). We are not even sure about the nature of the Carian script as yet. Bork held that it was mixture of an alphabetic (Greek)

Fig. 70. Carian inscription of Kaunos. (From Bossert, *Jahrbuch für kleinasiatische Forschung*, *I*, p. 331.)

and a syllabic (Cypriote?) writing, but nowadays Bossert is more inclined to call it a purely alphabetic system, not much more different from the Greek script than are the Lycian or Lydian alphabets.

So Carian still leaves an unknown quantity in Asia Minor, an area so rich in discoveries and positive results in the field of decipherments. Let us hope that it will not remain unknown forever.

4. The Indus Valley Script

Another system of writing about which we are still completely in the dark is the script appearing on a large number of seals and small copper plates found in Harappa (in the Punjab region of India) and lately in particular in Mohanjo-Daro in the Indus Delta. A few isolated specimens of this *Proto-Indic script*, customarily referred to as *Indus Valley script* or simply as *Indus script*, reached even Babylon, obviously in the course of trading, and Babylonian archeology succeeded in dating these inscriptions as originating about the middle of the third century B.C.

There seems to exist no possibility of deciphering this script either. The extreme brevity of the many inscriptions is a further obstacle. One of the hypotheses formulated is that these inscribed objects were brief seals or stamps used for administrative purposes (cf. Fig. 71). Nor is there any agreement concerning the number of the symbols; some scholars count as many as 400 different symbols, others not more than 150. Most investigators are of the opinion that this script is a mixture of ideograms and phonetic characters, perhaps syllabic signs.

The only serious work preparatory to a decipherment has been done by Meriggi; while he tries to interpret the alleged ideograms pictographically, he does not postulate any phonetic values. A more daring course was taken by Hrozný who tried to apply the same method to the Indus Valley script as to the Cretan writing, i.e., to decipher it on the ground of graphic similarities to the Hittite hieroglyphic writing. In this manner he claimed to deduce a great many phonetic values, which, however, as well as the conclusions he drew from them concerning a kinship of the Proto-Indians with the historically far younger "Hieroglyphic Hittites," are to be regarded as mere flights of fancy.

And one must regard likewise as a flight of fancy the attempt of Hevesy to establish links between this Proto-Indic script and the writing discovered on Easter Island, on the extreme eastern fringe of the Polynesian archipelago, basing his reasoning on the indubitably striking similarities in the shapes of characters of the very ancient Indus Valley script and those of the *Easter Island writing,* known merely from the last centuries, or rather from our very own era.

The Easter Island writing has been preserved on a number

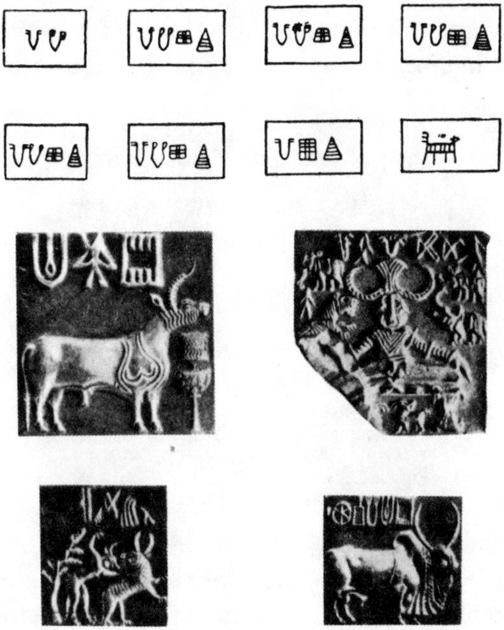

FIG. 71. Proto-Indic seals. (From Diringer, *The Alphabet*. Figs. 41 and 43.)

of wooden tablets, discovered on that island in and after 1870. Unfortunately, by that time none of the natives was able to read them, so that here we have an instance of an "undeciphered script of our own era." The pictographic symbols number about 500. They are so arranged on the tablets that the symbols in the alternate rows are always in inverted positions with respect to the symbols in both immediately adjacent rows, so that the reader had to turn the tablet upside down every time he finished reading a line (cf. Fig. 72). As a matter of fact, it is very doubtful even to what extent the use of the words "reader" and "reading" is justified here, i.e., to what extent, if at all, these tablets are written records, ideographically or phonetically written, of historical events, religious hymns, etc. It is possible that they were simply

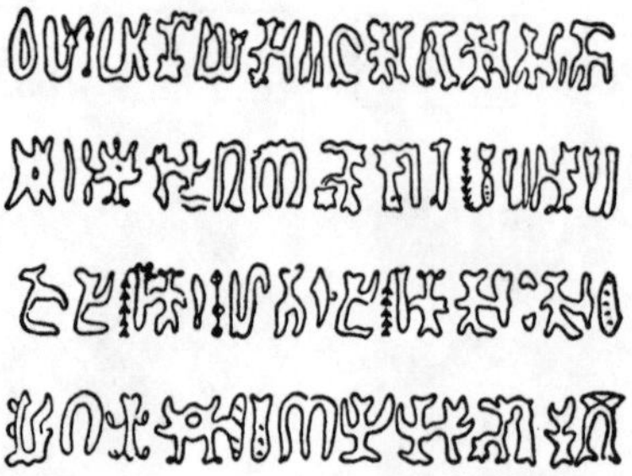

Fig. 72. The writing of Easter Island. (From Jensen, *Die Schrift*, Fig. 275.)

mnemonic devices in which each individual symbol was to remind the reader of an entire phrase, verse or section of a song, incantation, etc., like those employed by other primitive races. In any case, there is very little reason for hoping that we shall ever be able to reveal the meaning of these tablets of Easter Island.

To try to compare this almost totally unknown quantity of our own era with the Indus Valley script, separated from it by such a vast distance in space and above all in time, is in my opinion altogether too rash an attempt. The mere outward resemblance of the symbols, undeniable as it is (Fig. 73), is still no clue to their meanings or values, nor to the language and the contents of the texts written with them. He who does not believe in supernatural connections had better ascribe the outward similarity of the two scripts to mere coincidence.

Our survey thus concludes, seemingly unsatisfactorily, with a series of unanswered questions and fanciful conjectures. In my opinion, however, it would not have been right

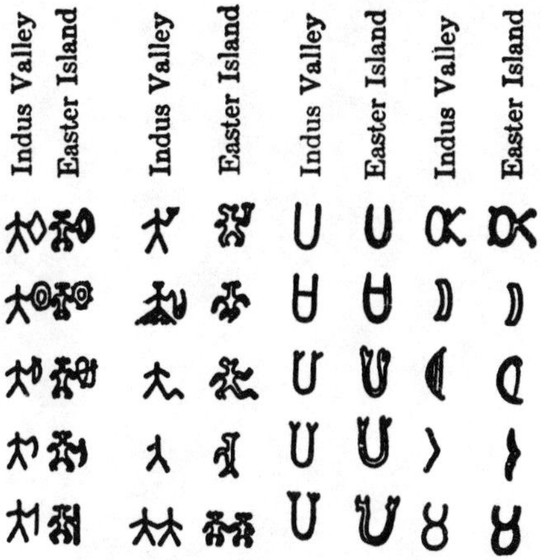

FIG. 73. The resemblance of the symbols of the Indus Valley script and of the Easter Island writing. (From Jensen, *Die Schrift*, Fig. 277.)

for me to present only the great accomplishments of decipherment and to disregard the still unsolved problems. It is always good to see not only the seemingly momentous achievements, but also the limitations of knowledge. After all, there still remains the hope that one day also these limitations will be overcome and the solution of the seemingly insoluble problems will be achieved.

APPENDIX

While the original German edition of this book was on the press, a very important accomplishment was made in the study of the writing of ancient Crete. Unless all appearances are deceptive, Michael Ventris, a young British architect, succeeded in deciphering the Cretan script known as *Linear Class B.* (cf. p. 164). We have learned, to our great surprise, that the language of these texts is an archaic form of the Achaean dialect of the *Greek language*, which thus was used not only in Pylos and Mycenae in Greece proper in the 13th century B.C., but also in Knossos, on the island of Crete, as far back as about 1400 B.C. Although the details of the study are still very far from being positively settled and the syllabary shown in Fig. 74, based on the latest accepted findings, is still likely to be changed further in the course of the next few years, the essential facts and general principles appear to be quite clearly established.

It can therefore be stated now that Linear Class B is composed of approximately 88 phonetic symbols, the phonetic value of almost all of which has been exactly established, and each and every one has been found to be a syllabic symbol representing an open syllable, i.e., a consonant followed by a vowel; furthermore, there are also a number of strongly pictographic word-signs, for "man," "woman," "horse," "war chariot," "tripod," etc., which may be regarded to a certain extent also as determinatives. The progress of the decipherment is impeded by the lack of bilingual texts, but is facilitated by the consistent separation of the individual words by strokes.

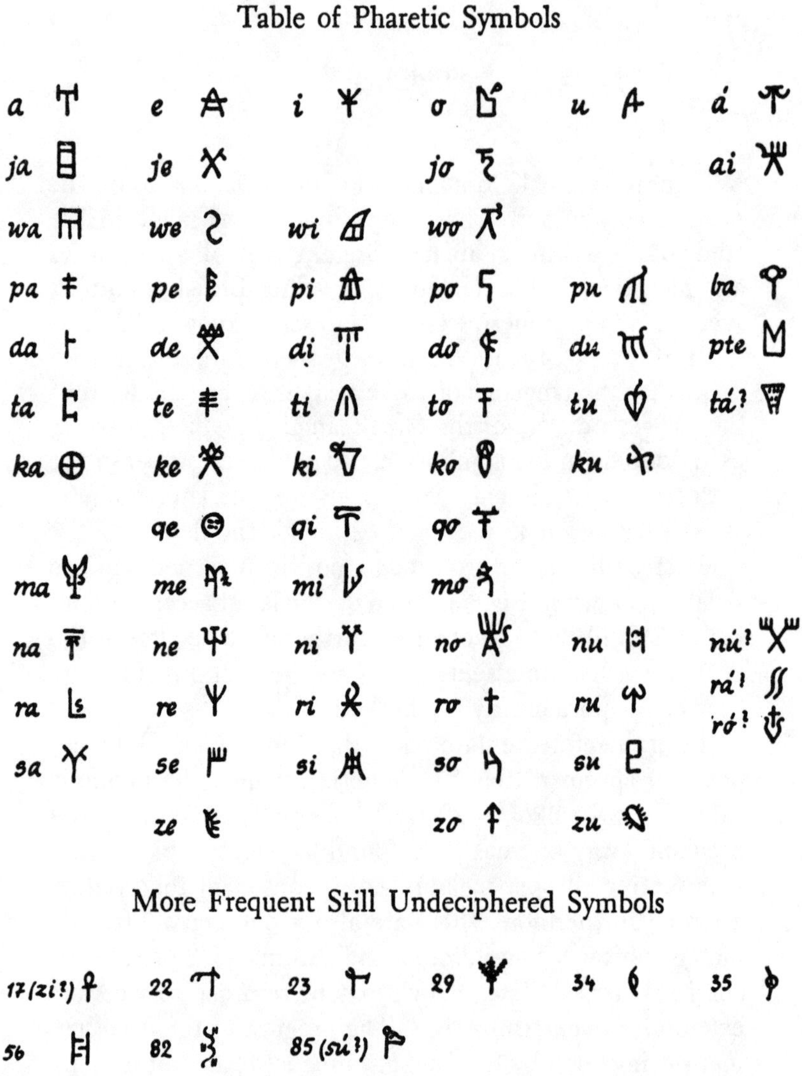
Table of Pharetic Symbols
a e i o u á
ja je jo ai
wa we wi wo
pa pe pi po pu ba
da de di do du pte
ta te ti to tu tá?
ka ke ki ko ku
qe qi qo
ma me mi mo
na ne ni no nu nú?
ra re ri ro ru rá? ró?
sa se si so su
ze zo zu
More Frequent Still Undeciphered Symbols
17 (zi?) 22 23 29 34 35
56 82 85 (sú?)

FIG. 74. Chart of the phonetic symbols of the Cretan Linear Class B script. (Meriggi in *Glotta* 34, 1954, p. 17.)

Ventris followed the example set by his predecessors, Sundwall, Kober and Sittig, in choosing the structure of the written words as the starting point for his decipherment, a method in general use also for breaking diplomatic codes and decoding secret writings. His conclusion that this was a syllabic script was reached on the ground of the number of the phonetic symbols, and of the analogy of the Cypriote syllabic writing. His immediate aim then was to arrange all the syllabic signs in a chess-board-like chart, in which every syllable beginning with the same *consonant* would appear in the same *horizontal row*, and all those ending in the same *vowel* in the same *vertical column*.

A very important task preliminary and preparatory to establishing definite syllabic values consisted in the exact determination of the various inflectional forms of the individual words; Alice Kober had done a great deal of painstaking detail work in that respect. She had recognized the fact that certain words, substantives according to the pictographic word-signs appearing next to them, appeared in three different case forms, but with their stems graphically unaltered. Likewise, the appended word-signs for "man" or "woman" made it possible to distinguish certain masculine words from the corresponding feminine ones by the different endings added to the unchanged stems. This is as though we distinguished the Italian *bam-bi-*NO ("boy") from *bam-bi-*NA ("girl") or *tut-*TO ("all"—masculine singular) from *tut-*TA ("all"—feminine singular) by different syllabic endings added to the same identical stem. In such a case, *no* and *na* would appear in the same horizontal row of the chess-board-like chart, *to* and *ta* would be in another horizontal row, whereas *no* and *to* would be found in one vertical column, and *na* and *ta* in another vertical column. The arranging of the syllable signs in the chart with maximum accuracy prior to the determination of their phonetic values was one of the most difficult tasks, but also one of those most important for the further progress of the research.

In establishing the phonetic values of the syllabic signs of Linear Class B, Ventris proceeded differently from the investigators before him, in that he completely disregarded the resemblance of the Cretan symbols to the signs of the well known Cypriote syllabary. He rather concentrated on recognizing *names* which would be good subjects for phonetic analysis. Male names could be recognized by the ideogram for "man" appended to them. Ventris assumed that certain groups of signs which occurred frequently suffixed to names of persons, were designations of *origin* and had to contain names of localities on Crete. Quite a few such place names were known, and judging by the number of the syllabic signs, a shorter, very frequently occurring group could be the name *Knossos*, a longer group the name *Amnisos*, etc. Making the best use of the chess-board-like chart, after wearisome experiments, Ventris then arrived at the chart of syllabic phonetic values shown, in its present state, in Fig. 74. The finding that in addition to the Cretan geographic names also Greek names of persons, as well as Greek names of deities, and even Greek words and inflectional forms were identified in the texts, was at first a surprise to the decipherer himself.

Of course, the Greek words are rendered in these texts in an oddly awkward manner, which goes far beyond the custom current in the Cypriote syllabic writing and appears to be an outright mutilation of the actual spoken forms. Since every sign stands for a syllable consisting of a consonant plus a vowel, and of no other pattern, difficulties arose first of all in the representation of two or more adjacent consonants. These difficulties were obviated either by the graphic interpolation of mute vowels (writing *ko-no-so* for *Knossos*, *a-mi-ni-so* for *Amnisos*) or by writing only one of two adjacent consonants (e.g., *pa-i-to* for *Phaistos*). In syllables ending in *l*, *m*, *n*, *r* or *s*, the script did not indicate these final sounds at all, nor did it indicate the *i* of any *i*-diphthong. In other words, the users of this script wrote *po-me* for *poimén* ("shepherd"), *i-yo-te* for *ióntes* ("those who go"), *ka-ke-u* for *khalkeús* ("blacksmith"), and the nominative singular *kórvos* ("young man"), the accusative singular *kórvon* as well as the nominative plural *kórvoi* fused in writing in the single form *ko-vo*. Thus, a given written word or phrase can be read and of course also translated in very different ways. Consequently, a considerable degree of uncertainty will have to be taken into account with reference to all future translations of texts written in the Linear Class B script.

It seems, however, to be indicated to present a few arguments to demonstrate that the decipherment progress is on the right path and the uncertainties are to be attributed primarily to the imperfection of the script. The Greek *trípūs* ("tripod") occurs in one text first in the singular form, *ti-ri-po* = *trípūs*, and is accompanied by the picture of a tripod, as a word-sign or determinative, and the figure 1, whereas in another place it appears in the dual, *ti-ri-po-de* = *trípode* = "two tripods," accompanied by the same pictogram and the numeral 2. The same text contains also the word *dépas* ("goblet") with various qualifiers: In one instance, we see *di-pa me-vi-yo ti-ri-yo-ve* = *dípas mevion triốves* = "a smaller, three-eared (three-handled) goblet," with the picture of a three-handled goblet and the numeral 1; we find also *di-pa me-vi-yo qe-to-ro-ve* = *dípas mevion qetr-ốves* = "a smaller, four-eared goblet," with the picture of a four-handled goblet and the numeral 1; there occurs the phrase *di-pa-e me-zo-e ti-ri-o-ve-e* = *dípae mézoe tri-ốvee* = "two larger, three-eared goblets," with the picture of a three-handled goblet and the numeral 2; and finally, there is the particularly pretty *di-pa me-vi-yo a-no-ve* = *dípas mevion an-ốves* = "a smaller, earless goblet," with the picture of a goblet without handle and the numeral 1. In my opinion, all these findings are striking arguments for the correctness of the decipherment of Ventris.

Whereas Linear Class B is thus revealed as Greek, Linear Class A seems to be non-Greek and, like the Cretan pictographic writing, defies all attempts at decipherment for the time being.

INDEX

Ahaz, 32
Akerblad, 19
Akkadian cuneiform writing (Babylonian-Assyrian), 3, 4, 29–44, 45, 48, 51, 52, 59, 60–68, 70, 71, 72, 73, 74, 79, 80, 81, 82, 83, 85, 86, 90, 91, 132, 153, 155
Alexander the Great, 2, 4, 18, 30, 32
Alexandrinus, Clemens, 5
Amasis, 4
Amenemhet III, 2
Amenophis III, 3, 24
Amenophis IV, 3
Amosis, 3
Arabic writing, 63, 67, 123
Aramaic language, 49, 110–114
Arkwright, 108
Armenian language, 95
Arrian, 115
Assarhaddon, 32
Assurbanipal, 32
Avestic language, 56, 58, 59
Babylonion-Assyrian language, *see* Akkadian
Basque language, 139
Bauer, Hans, 83–84, 131, 162
Behistun Inscription, 58–59, 65
Berber language, 123
Bilalama, 33
Birch, 25, 129
Blumenthal, von, 146
Bork, 130, 168
Bosch, 116
Bossert, 97, 98–99, 116–117, 169
Botta, 60, 64
Brandenstein, Carl Georg von, 80
Brandis, Johannes, 130
Brugsch, Heinrich, 25
Budge, 26
Bugge, 108
Burnouf, 57
Cambyses, 55
Carian script, 167–169
Caucasian languages, 109, 139
Caylus, Count, 51
Celtic language, 144
Chabas, 26
Champollion, Jean François, 17, 19–25, 53, 63, 93
Chardin, 51
Charlemagne, 30
Chefren, 2
Cheops, 2
Chinese writing, 8, 16, 29, 35, 70
Collitz-Bechtel, 126
Coptic language, 11, 21, 22
Cowley, 97
Cretan-Minoan script, 34, 157, 163–167, 170, 178, 180
Cypriote-Greek writing, 124–131, 165–166, 177, 178
Cyrus, 32, 55, 63
Darius, 44, 48, 54, 56, 58, 62, 63, 154
Deecke, 130
Delitzsch, Friedrich, 67
Della Valle, Pietro, 51
Dhorme, 84, 131, 134–136
Dunand, M., 133
Dutch language, 143
Early Egyptian, 18, 24, 26
Early Persian writing, 44, 48, 49, 50–59, 60, 83, 154
Early Turkish runic writing, 123
Easter Island writing, 170–173
Egyptian demotic writing, 7, 18
Egyptian hieratic writing, 5–6
Egyptian hieroglyphic writing, x, xi, 1–29, 34, 35, 39, 44, 51, 86, 90, 91, 95, 102, 132, 152, 153, 159, 160, 162, 165
Elamite language, 35, 44, 52, 82–83
English words, 12 156
Epiphanes, Ptolemy, 18
Erman, Adolph, 24, 26
Erman-Ranke, 4
Etruscan language, 114, 137–143, 146, 151, 154, 155, 156, 166
Falkenstein, 69
Finnish language, 70
Forrer, 97
Frank, Carl, 97
Friedländer, 115
Gardiner, 26, 160–162
Gelb, 97
German language, 143, 144, 145, 146, 156
Gothic language, 146
Greek alphabet, 11, 21, 27, 104, 147
Greek language, x, 18–24, 75, 91, 105–117, 124–131, 139, 145, 146–150, 166, 167, 169, 174–180
Greek language, modern, 156
Griffith, 27
Grimme, H., 136, 162
Grotefend, Georg Friedrich, 53–59, 62, 63, 93, 154
Gudea of Lagash, 30
Haas, O., 149, 150
Hammurabi, 30, 31, 33, 68
Hattušili III, 4, 47
Hebrew language, x, 63, 67
Heeren, 57
Herbig, 114, 143
Herodotus, 51, 55, 114, 154
Hesychos, 130
Hevesy, 170
Hincks, Edward, 25, 58, 64, 66
Hinz, 82
Hittite cuneiform writing, 35, 38, 39, 45–47, 69–79, 86, 90, 93, 97, 102, 109, 115, 151–152, 155, 165
Hittite hieroglyphic writing, xi, 47, 70, 71, 86–101, 102, 152, 153–154, 157, 170
Homer, x
Horapollon, 17
Hoseah, 32
Hrozný, Friedrich, 70, 74, 75, 76, 97, 98, 157–158, 165, 170
Hungarian Language, 70
Hurrian Language, 35, 45, 46, 79–81, 84
Hystaspes, 56, 63, 154
Illyrian Language, 144, 145
Imbert, 108
Indilumma, 92
Indo-European Languages, ix, 44, 45, 46, 47, 70, 74, 75, 78, 86, 90, 95, 101, 108, 109, 114, 143, 144, 146, 147, 148, 150, 166
Indus Valley script, 157, 158, 169–173
Italic Languages, 139, 140, 143, 144, 146, 149
Japanese writing, 16, 70
Jensen, 81, 95–97
Kahle, 114
Kalinka, E., 104–105
Kämpfer, Engelbert, 51